the

AmericanSandbox™

DICTIONARY

of

CHILDREN'S
MISPRONOUNCED
ENGLISH

To Jane & James.

Best Wishes,

By **Alvin Zamudio**

REEDY PRESS
St. Louis, Missouri

Reedy Press
PO Box 5131
St. Louis, MO 63139, USA

Library of Congress Control Number: 2010933584

ISBN: 978-1-933370-63-7

Please visit our website at www.reedypress.com.

Illustrated by Addison and Mya Zamudio.

Printed in the United States of America
10 11 12 13 14   5 4 3 2 1

To all the children in our world who have no
parents to hear their mispronounced words
and laugh with them in love

Contents

Acknowledgments

I first would like to thank my faithful wife, Margaret, for not only encouraging me to pursue this project and for putting in countless hours going through emails and entering submissions into the database, but also for taking care of our family, which allowed me the much needed mental freedom to work.

My two oldest children, Addison and Mya, must also be thanked for their hard-working imaginations while illustrating many of these definitions. Next is my friend Stan Green who years ago would chastise me to compile this book every time he saw me. Even though it took me a decade to act on it, I fear I would have forsaken it altogether if not for his regular exhortation.

I also would like to thank Angel James and John Pertzborn of Fox 2 St. Louis for giving me my first TV appearance; my publishers Josh Stevens and Matthew Heidenry of Reedy Press for investing in me; Mike Hammock of shorcutsolutions.net for the support in both friendship and marketing; my old friend Neal Brown for brainstorming and creative moral support; Jennifer Labit of Cotton Babies, our true hero of the hour who alerted her entire customer email list of remaining room for submissions to help us meet our final goal for this first edition; the charter members of the "Word Squad" group on Facebook; the faithful members of the Facebook fan page; and all our friends and family who encouraged me, submitted words, and took time out of their lives to help "spread the words" by posting and sharing definitions online and via email to generate more interest.

My greatest acknowledgments, of course, go to both the children who spoke these mispronounced words and to their caring parents who took the time to submit them to us. As long as kids around the country keep trying to master this rather complex language of ours and their loving parents keep sending us the words, future editions of this book are always a possibility. Thanks to each and every one of you for making this possible for me and my family. I am honored and forever grateful.

Foreword

It all started with one word.

One rainy day when my niece Jamie was around eight years old, I came to her house to take her and her little brothers, Andy and Aaron, out for some time together and to give their mother a break. As we approached the front door to leave, Jamie all of a sudden stopped and said, "Uncle Alvin, it's raining outside! Don't forget your bulella!" After a few days of mulling over her innocent gaff, I began to imagine a "dictionary" of all the funny mispronunciations children say in the English language. People could read through them and celebrate the humor and innocence of childhood. I kept the idea in my head until 1995 when I revisited it again and decided to put a formal manuscript together. After contacting my sister, Irma, and a few other friends who had children (I was not even married at the time) to collect more words, I sat down at a computer and worked out some funny definitions. This is how *The American Sandbox Dictionary of Children's Mispronounced English* was born.

My idea only went so far. With the Internet still a new frontier and with no experience as a writer or knowledge of publishing, I simply printed out what I had and kept it in my repertoire in case something ever "came up." In 1998 I told my friend Stan Green about the idea, who took it upon himself to sternly remind me to "write that book" every chance he could, both because he knew its potential and because he loved children. He and his wife, Regina, are two of the best, most patient, and faithful parents I had ever had the pleasure to meet. They had chosen only to parent adopted children. This honorable act of love and Stan's constant reminders are among the many reasons I have committed to giving at least a tenth of the profits of this book to support orphaned children.

In 2002 I finally married, and my wife, Margaret, and I had three little ones of our own. Over the years, as their own mispronunciations emerged, the smoldering wick of the dictionary started to get good air. By 2009 I had enough kindling to ignite into a flame. By that time, I had gained much experience designing and building websites, so I decided to try my hand using the Internet to solicit more words. After staying up all night laboring through fresh inspiration, I had a basic site put together with a logo, a simple explanation of the idea, an email form for submissions, and one word: "bulella." I then did my best to gather some of the old words, a few new ones from current friends and family, and some of my own kids' words, and I launched the site.

Even though I had this idea for many years, it still needed refining. I quickly discovered that I was on my own. For starters, there were groups and tips online for just about anything, except for how to write a dictionary. Surprisingly, there was not even a single site I could find that dealt with kids mispronouncing words, except how to help correct them and a couple of forums where parents shared funny words and stories among other topics. I also needed to let people know about the site, but because of limited funds I could not afford paid ads, and forums were very strict on soliciting websites. During this time, both my wife and I had been accumulating a number of friends both old and new on Facebook, so I figured that would be the best place to push. So with the help of friends, membership to a few parenting groups, the ability to start my own fan page for the dictionary, and offering credit for the child who mispronounced the word, things actually began to move. Within a few weeks, the process developed into a regular system. I would review the emailed submissions from the site, decide on the best ones, write a definition that had a bit of humor to it (especially as it relates to the world of children), post it on the site, and then share it all over Facebook, which not only led to great interest but also to more submissions.

Later that year, I heeded a suggestion to send out a press release to local television stations for possible interviews. I had about sixty-five strong words on the site so I figured I was ready to meet the press. One station responded, and I was asked to go on the morning show for an interview. The interview went smoothly, and I came home to more than three hundred submissions waiting for me in my inbox. The real coup, however, was that John Pertzborn, who interviewed me on the show, offered me a couple of contacts for local publishers he knew, one of whom was Josh Stevens at Reedy Press.

So even though it took many years for this book to come to pass, I can now see how this benefited the project. Aside from advances in the technology and communication that have made the process of developing this idea much simpler, I am also very proud to have my first book illustrated by my children! Their drawings are so fitting because they provide one more angle on the same innocent perception that brought about each mispronounced word they illustrated. And the time I was able to spend with them—working out details and fixing mistakes—will now be a great memory for us to revisit every time we read this book.

On a deeper level, the greatest asset that time gave to this book was that I became more qualified to write it. As an older man and an experienced father of young children, I was able to see how this book could be enlightening as well as entertaining, which gave me great insight not only into word selection but also in how better to write their definitions.

Additional time also helped me see the dictionary's huge potential to aid parents and those who work with children in a way I never previously realized. I discovered that each of these mispronounced words not only offers us a glimpse into our children's little worlds and demonstrates their healthy desire to be in ours, but they also can inspire us to interact more with our children and heighten our connectivity. I realized this when I found myself paying more attention to what my kids were saying, which meant I was paying more attention to them. Other parents told me they were starting to do the same. In such a busy world as ours, only good can come from that.

So now you hold in your hands the realization of a dream that was literally years in the making, and well worth the wait. My niece Jamie is now married and raising her own firstborn child. And after all this time it is hard to believe that what she inspired in me with just one mispronounced word so long ago has finally come to pass, but I am so thankful it has and am excited that others finally can share in the results. May you enjoy reading this book as much as I did writing and compiling it. May you also enjoy the journal pages we have added at the end of the book where you can record the mispronounced words you hear from the children in your life. But most importantly may all that is contained within these pages remind you that some mistakes children make are better celebrated than corrected because they keep fresh in your heart the joy and wonders of childhood.

—Alvin Zamudio

A

ac·ci·dent [AK-sih-dehnt] *noun*

A notably distinct or unique difference in articulation, tone, or inflection of spoken language by comparison to one's own style of speech, which often varies depending on a person's region or nationality.

*"My Aunt Mary has an English **accident**."*

—Cleo, age 4, San Diego, CA

ad·je·lust [add-juh-LUHST] *verb*

To arrange or fit into place, usually to increase or restore order, such as rearranging books on a shelf, adapting to new surroundings, or performing actions to alleviate physical pain or discomfort.

*"Daddy, did the chiropractor **adjelust** your back?"*

—Bree, age 3, Raleigh, NC

a·dor·a·bub·ble [ah-DORE-uh-buh-bl] *noun*

Exceptionally charming or delightful.

*"Mom, I'm **adorabubble**!"*

—Macia, age 3, Bellingham, WA

a·gil·la·tor [AH-jil-lay-tur] *noun*

A large reptile, native to the wetland areas of China and the southeastern United States, characterized by its long broad mouth, sharp teeth, and powerful jaws.

*"**Agillators** can crush anything when they bite!"*

Also pronounced *atticeater*.

—Jada, age 3, Alton, IL. Additional source: Candice, age 2, St. Peters, MO

air con·dic·ity [AYRE kun-diss-ih-tee] *noun*

A system that reduces the temperature, controls the humidity, and ventilates an atmosphere, such as the interior of a home or a vehicle.

*"Mom, it's hot in here! Can you please turn on the **air condicity**?"*

—Jack, age 4, Omaha, NB

air·punk [AYRE-puhnk] *noun*

A device that forces air into an object by manual or mechanical compression such as a flat bicycle tire.

*"Dad, you better get the **airpunk**!"*

—Eddie, age 4, Clearfield, UT

a·lam·ba·lance [ah-LAM-buh-luns] *noun*

An emergency vehicle that transports sick or injured people, usually equipped with flashing lights and a siren and drives fast.

*"Dad, can we buy an **alambalance** instead of a new minivan?"*

Also pronounced *ambliance* and *ambyents*.

—Patrick, age 4, Las Cruces, NM. Additional sources: Ella, age 2, UK; Janice, age 5, MO; Erin, age 3, Bramptom, Ontario, Canada

Al·an's ap·ple [AHL-enz a-puhl] *noun*

A nickname from Judeo-Christian society, derived from its traditional belief of the name of the first created man, given to the thyroid cartilage at the front of the human neck that is typically more visible in men than in women.

*"Dad, why don't girls have an **Alan's apple**?"*

—Kelly, age 3

Al·ba·nan·a [Al-buh-NAHN-uh] *proper noun*

A state in the southeastern United States with a partial coastline on the Gulf of Mexico, with the city of Montgomery as its capital.

*"We live in **Albanana**!"*

—Cyrus, age 4, Mobile, AL

Alf·can·dy·land [ahlf-KAN-dee-land] *noun*

A republic of central Asia, with the city of Kabul as its capital.

"Mom, when is Uncle Trevor coming home from Alfcandyland?"

—Danielle, age 3, Roseville, CA

Alfcandyland

After learning that my brother-in-law was being deployed to Afghanistan for nearly a year, my husband and I were very worried and discussed it quite a bit, not thinking our three-year-old daughter, Danielle, was paying attention. When she came up and asked me one day, "Mom, when is Uncle Trevor coming home from Alfcandyland?" We loved this sweet little twist and have only called it Alfcandyland ever since.

—Gina, Roseville, CA

---

all rot·ten [ahl RAH-tehn] *adjective*

Topped with grated cheese and sometimes bread crumbs or butter, and then baked until browned.

*"Mom makes great potatoes **all rotten**!"*

—Ashlee, age 5, St. Peters, MO

al·vin·but·ter [AL-vihn-buh-tur] *noun*

An edible paste or spread made from ground almonds.

*"Dad, can I have some more **alvinbutter** on my sandwich?"*

—Sean, age 3, St. Louis, MO

a·mer·i·ca-go-round

[ah-MEHR-ih-kuh-gowe-rownd] *noun*

A revolving amusement park ride with seats in the form of horses and other animals.

*"The **america-go-round** makes me dizzy!"*

—Lucy, age 4, St. Louis, MO

an·ni·ver·si·ty [AN-ih-vehr-sih-tee] *noun*

The yearly occurrence of a past event that is commemorated or celebrated on or around the same date, such as a wedding.

*"Mom and Dad are going out for their **anniversity!**"*

—Ava, age 5, Cheyenne, WY

an·nor·ing [uh-NOR-eeng] *adjective*

1. Causing irritation, such as a child who antagonizes his siblings.

2. Choosing not to notice or pay attention to, such as a child who, after being told not to antagonize his siblings, no longer responds to or interacts with them out of spite.

*"Mommy, Teddy's **annoring** me!"*

—Madie Grace, age 4, Memphis, TN

ap·pen·dem·ic [ah-pehn-DEHM-ik] *noun*

A disease or condition rapidly affecting many people at one time, such as an infection or a virus.

*"The black plague was an **appendemic**!"*

—Ethan, age 6, Bristol, TN

ap·pe·tize·ment [AH-puh-tyez-mehnt] *noun*

An audible or visual announcement, such as a television commercial or a billboard, of goods or services sold.

*"I saw an **appetizement** for the toy I want!"*

—Hannah, age 5, Louisville, KY

ap·ple spi·der [A-puhl spye-dr] *noun*

A juice made from pressed apples, sometimes sweetened with sugar or spiced with cinnamon, that can be served chilled or heated.

*"Mom, can I have more hot **apple spider?**"*

—Jeremy, age 3, Topeka, KS

ap·ple·at·us [A-puhl-AT-uhs] *noun*

A collection or group of objects intended for a specific purpose, such as playground equipment intended for children's play.

*"A swingset is an **appleatus!**"*

—Stephanie, age 4, Burlington, VT

ap·ple·lu·cy [A-puhl-LOO-see] *adverb*

Positively or certainly; without exception.

*"You're **applelucy** right, Mom!"*

—Milo, age 3, Bloomsburg, PA

ap·ple·puss [A-puhl-puhss] *noun*

A cephalopod mollusk of the order *Octopoda*, having eight sucker-bearing arms, a soft, oval-shaped body, and strong beak-like jaws that lives primarily at the bottom of the sea.

*"Daddy, if we lived in the ocean, could I ride an **applepuss**?"*

—Lars, age 2, Moorhead, MN

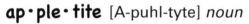

ap·ple·tite [A-puhl-tyte] *noun*

A craving or need for nourishment, such as food or drink, which can also refer to other desires, such as a strong interest in a favorite activity.

*"I have an **appletite** for books!"*

—Maya, age 4, San Antonio, TX

---

ap·ple·toss [A-puhl-taws] *noun*

A soft pulp made from stewed apples that is often sweetened and sometimes spiced with cinnamon.

*"I want more **appletoss**, please!"*

—Thomas, 19 months, PA

ar·ki·choke [ARR-kih-chohk] *noun*

A European vegetable with thistle-like leaves that form a flowery head, parts of which can be eaten, such as in salads or other foods, or used in condiments.

*"Mom is making **arkichoke** dip!"*

—Gabriel, age 2, St. Louis, MO

arm·pips [AHRM-pips] *plural noun*

The areas, which have a tendency to emit strong odor, beneath the intersection of the arms and shoulders.

*"Uncle Adam needs to take a shower because his **armpips** stink!"*

Also pronounced *armchops.*

—Lily, age 4, Sappington, MO. Additional source: Angela, 16 months, FL

as·car·y·gus [uh-SKAIR-ee-guhs] *noun*

A plant with edible shoots that most children instinctively will not eat.

*"I don't care what it tastes like, I hate **ascarygus**!"*

—Donna, age 3, Fenton, MO

as·pol·o·gize [az-POL-uh-jize] *verb*

To make a formal defense or admit to fault.

*"Sarah, I **aspologize** for painting your dog."*

—Addison, age 6, St. Louis, MO

As·trayn·ia [ahs-TRAYN-yah] *proper noun*

A continent in the Southwestern Pacific Ocean, Southeast of Asia, and bordering the Indian Ocean, known in part for its unique wildlife.

*"Kangaroos are from **Astraynia**!"*

—Jesse, age 5, Bellevue, WA

av·a·da·ca·do [av-ah-duh-KAH-doh] *noun*

A pear-shaped, tropical fruit with a green or black skin, a light green pulp, and a single seed, popular in dips and salads but typically detested by children.

"I hate avadacado!"

Also pronounced *bacado*.

—Emma, age 5, Tallahassee, FL. Additional source: Alejandro, age 4, Houston, TX

av·er·ga·ting [AHV-uhr-gay-ting] *adjective*

Causing unwanted or intolerable tension or stress.

"Jimmy is so avergating!"

—Katie, age 2, St. Louis, MO

aw·ffles [AWW-fuhls] *plural noun*

Small batter cakes known for their grid-like design, cooked in an iron or toasted, and typically served at breakfast with syrup, powdered sugar, and other creative, tasty toppings.

"Mom, can I have ice cream on my awffles today?"

—Pamela, age 12, St. Louis, MO

ba·by suit [BAY-bee soot] *noun*

A garment worn for swimming or bathing, often decorated with patterns or creative designs.

*"Mom got me a new **babysuit** with flowers on it!"*

Also pronounced *babysoup.*

—Colette, age 3, Bothell, WA.
Additional source: Sean, age 3, Mobile, AL

ba·by·o·li [bay-bee-OH-lee] *noun*

Small pieces of square or round pasta, stuffed with meat, cheese, or other fillings, typically served in a tomato-based sauce or breaded and baked.

*"Can I have **babyoli** for dinner?"*

—Kali, age 5, East Alton, IL

back · yoon [bak-YUNE] *noun, verb*

1. A space completely devoid of matter.

2. A machine that uses mechanical power to remove matter from surfaces with suction.

3. What people usually have to do when children eat chips or cookies unsupervised.

*"Uh oh, Mom! Better get the **backyoon**!"*

—Jocelyn, age 2, Bridgeton, MO

bad · gam · mon [BAHD-gahm-muhn] *noun*

A two-player board game in which both players move their pieces around triangular points on the board in accordance to a throw of dice, competing to be the first to remove all of their pieces from the board.

*"I can play **badgammon**!"*

—Lillian, age 4, Cedar Rapids, IA

ba·jan·ya [buh-JAHN-ya] *noun*

A "private part" of the female (Mommy) anatomy from which babies are born.

"I came from my Mommy's bajanya!"

Also pronounced *regina*.

—Jody, age 4, Summerville, SC. Additional source: Evelyn, age 5, Saskatchewan, Canada

---

Private Question

I had to stop myself from laughing when my four-year-old daughter, Lindsay, and I were both in the bathroom one day after a swimming party and as I was changing she stopped, pointed, and asked, "Mommy, why do you have fur down there?" What a time I had explaining that one!

—Meridith, Jacksonville, FL

---

ba·lax·ing [buh-LAKKS-eeng] *adjective*

To relieve or lessen stress, tension, or rigidity, such as to sit on a comfortable piece of furniture.

"This chair is so balaxing!"

—Michael, age 4, Fayetteville, AR

bam·mer [BAM-r] *noun, verb*

1. A tool with a solid head set atop a handle that is used to hit other objects such as wood, metal, or nails. The tool can be quite destructive when used on surfaces or objects they are not intended for.

"Dad, I accidentally broke the TV with your **bammer**."

2. The act of using any object to pound another.

*"Do you want me to **bammer** the TV some more to fix it?"*

—Wolfgang, age 3, Nashville, TN

ba·nan·a spit [buh-NAN-ah spiht] *noun*

A famous American dessert served with ice cream on a banana sliced lengthwise and topped with fruit, flavored syrup, whipped cream, and nuts.

*"I want a **banana spit** with chocolate ice cream!"*

Also called *nana spit*.

—Jerry, age 4, Houston, TX. Additional source: Benjamin, age 3, Clarendon, TX

bath·tize [BATH-tyze] *verb*

The traditionally Christian rite during which one is immersed in or sprinkled with water as a symbol of spiritual cleansing that can also appear quite similar to the act of physical cleansing.

*"Mom, I have school tomorrow so don't you need to **bathtize** me?"*

—Dennis, age 7, St. Louis, MO

ba·zan·ya [buh-ZAHN-ya] *noun*

A baked Italian pasta dish usually consisting of three to four layers of pasta, cheese, ground beef, and a red tomato-based sauce.

*"We're having **bazanya** tonight!"*

Also pronounced *panzania*.

—Bailey, age 4, Summerville, SC. Additional source: Kaylee, age 4, Ladera Ranch, CA

berf·day [BEHRF-daye] *noun*

The anniversary of a person's birth, typically celebrated by a social festivity such as a gathering where cake and ice cream are served, and consummated by the time-honored custom of presenting gifts to the honoree.

*"Look what I got for my **berfday**!"*

—Margaret, age 3, St. Peters, MO

be·zert [beh-ZURT] *noun*

The traditionally last course of a meal that is usually sweet, also known universally to be the most important part of any meal to children.

*"Can I have **bezert** now?"*

—Lillian, age 7, Springfield, OH

blank light [BLAYNK lyte] *noun*

An electric lamp that emits virtually invisible infrared or ultraviolet light, causing white or other bright colors to be more illuminated than darker colors.

*"My shoes and shirt were glowing in the **blank light**!"*

—Stewart, age 5, Martinsville, IN

blank steak [BLAYNK stayk] *noun*

A cut of meat from the side of an animal, typically attributed to beef.

*"Are we having **blank steak** for dinner again?!"*

—Mya, age 5, St. Louis, MO

block·mus·tard [BLOK-mus-tird] *proper noun*

1. A nickname for aerial demolition bombs that also became a common reference for a widely successful motion picture.

2. A corporation started in Texas in 1985 that rents movies for home viewing, including films for children.

*"Dad, it's Friday! Can we go to **blockmustard**?"*

—Leah, age 3, St. Louis, MO

blue·ba·by [BLOO-baye-bee] *noun*

An edible fruit with a distinct blue color and a semi-sweet flavor that is often used in or to flavor food, such as muffins or snow cones.

*"Make mine **bluebaby**, please!"*

—Lucas, age 2, Watertown, MA

bluff [BLUHF] *verb*

To clean or polish a surface for a flat, grainless finish, typically what is needed for any optical media, such as a DVD if left in the possession of children without proper supervision.

*"Dad, you need to **bluff** my movie again because it won't play."*

—Addison, age 6, Ferguson, MO

bo·a con·trac·tor [bow-uh kohn-TRAK-tr] *noun*

A large snake of the family *Boa* that is native to tropical regions of the Americas, such as the anaconda or the python, that coils around and suffocates its prey.

*"That scarf looks like a **boa contractor**!"*

—Danny, age 6, Baltimore, MD

boil·er [BOYL-r] *noun*

A device that cooks food such as meat, fish, or poultry by direct heat, typically a function of a conventional kitchen oven.

*"Mom makes steaks in the **boiler**!"*

—Stephan, age 5, Miami, FL

Booger King [BOOHG-r keeng] *proper noun*

An American fast food restaurant established in 1953 by Keith J. Kramer and Matthew Burns that specializes in preparing flame-broiled burgers that have since become internationally known.

*"We're having lunch at **Booger King**!"*

Also pronounced *King Booger*.

—Sarah Mae, age 4, Memphis, TN. Additional source: Ben, age 5, Tallahassee, FL

brace·slip [BRASE-slip] *noun*

A band, string, or chain worn on the wrist or ankle typically for cosmetic decoration, unless you go to the hospital, where they put your name on it.

*"When I get better can I take this **braceslip** off?"*

—Ethan, age 4, Canada

breeth·case [BREETH-kayse] *noun*

A typically flat carrying case with a handle and locks that adults keep important things in, usually for work.

*"Oh no! Dad forgot his **breethcase!**"*

—Danna, age 3, St. Louis, MO

bref·kissed [BREF-kist] *noun*

The first and most important meal of the day, portions of which are known to stick to children more than any other meal.

*"Mom, can I have pancakes and syrup for **brefkissed**."*

—Ty, age 3, Brampton, Ontario, Canada

bris·ket [BRIHS-keht] *noun*

A small bread leavened with baking powder, baking soda, or yeast, with a flaky outer crust and soft interior, typically served as a side for meals and often spread with butter or preserves.

*"Can I have jelly on my **brisket?**"*

—Halina, age 4, San Antonio, TX

bub·loon [buhb-LOON] *noun*

An inflatable sack of light material that can be filled with a gas that is lighter than air, causing it to float. It is often suspended by a ribbon or line of string, which is not always an effective solution when left in the hands of children.

*"Mommy, my **bubloon** is floating away again!"*

—Tommy, age 2, NJ

bu·lel·la [buh-LEHL-ah] *noun*

An expanding canopy device held over the head to protect against sun or rain.

*"Uncle Alvin, don't forget your **bulella** because it's raining outside!"*

Also pronounced *umbranella*, *rainbrella*, and *funbrella*.

—Jamie, age 8, St. Charles, MO. Additional sources: Max, age 4, Alton, IL; Sean, age 5, O'Fallon, IL; Ella, age 3, Urbana, IL; Brady, age 3, Friendswood, TX

bull·zo·dor [BOOL-zoe-dr] *noun*

A powerful treaded machine with a broad, vertically concaved blade at its front that is used for clearing earth or debris.

*"They had to get a **bullzoder** to move it all!"*

—Jordan, age 3, Saint John, New Brunswick, Canada

bum·ble·gum [BUHM-bl-guhm] *noun*

A type of chewing gum with an elastic consistency that allows it to be blown into large bubbles that can sometimes get stuck to many things.

*"Mom, Jimmy got his **bumblegum** in my hair!"*

Also pronounced *gobblegum*.

—Jada, age 4, Alton, IL. Additional source: Benedicte, age 2, Washington, D.C.

bur·gu·lar [BERHG-yoo-lr] *noun*

A person who trespasses, usually by forced entry, on to another person's premises with intent to steal their posessions.

*"Dad, what if a **burgular** breaks in?!"*

—Andy, age 5, Gordon, NSW, Australia

bus·cif·ul·lo [buhs-KIF-uh-low] *noun, proper noun*

1. A large, wild oxen, from the *Bovidae* family, also known as bison.

2. A city in the state of New York after which is named a unique hot sauce for fried chicken wings, which may understandably confuse children.

*"You mean **buscifullo** don't fly?"*

—Cedric, age 3, Crestwood, MO

bus·ket·ti [bus-KEH-tee] *noun*

A long, starchy Italian pasta that is sometimes served with meatballs.

*"Dad's making **busketti** tonight!"*

Also pronounced *basghetti, psketti, sketty, skabetty,* and *spunitty.*

—Joe, age 5, St. Louis, MO; Pamela, age 4, Biddeford, ME. Additional sources: Easton, age 5, Phoenix, AZ; Alexander, age 4, St. Louis, MO

buz·zas·ter [buh-ZAHSS-tr] *noun*

An event that causes great loss, damage, or hardship such as an earthquake or a child's room after playtime.

*"Mom says my room is a **buzzaster!**"*

—Kelli, age 6, Berlin, NH

Baby in the Tummy

While at the store one day, my three-year-old daughter, Julia, noticed a pregnant lady and asked her why her stomach was so big. The lady told her there was a baby in there. Julia must have thought about it and shortly after asked me, "Mommy, why did that lady eat her baby?"

—Irma, St. Louis, MO

---

cal·a·cal·a·cow [Kahl-a-kahl-a-KAHW] *noun*

A large reptile of the family *Crocodylidae*, native to the tropical areas of Africa, Asia, the Americas, and Australia, with a long mouth, sharp teeth, and a unique textured skin for which it has been extensively hunted.

*"Look Mom, that man's boots look like a **calacalacow**!"*

—Colette, age 2, Bothell, WA

can·dice [KAN-diss] *noun*

A heavy woven cloth made of cotton, hemp, or linen that is used for making tents, sails, or as a painting surface; also any article of children's clothing used for the same purpose.

*"Look Mom, I can use my shirt as a **candice**!"*

—Mya, age 5, Ferguson, MO

can·dy·gar·den [KAN-dee-gahr-den] *noun*

Traditionally the first formal class of school for children between four and six years of age.

*"When I turn five I'll go to **candygarden**!"*

—Annie, age 3, St. Louis, MO

can·te·lope [KAN-tl-ohp] *noun*

An animal from the *Bovidae* family, native to Africa and Asia, with long, hollow, unbranched horns.

*"Look Grandma! There's a **cantelope**!"*

—Alix, age 2, St. Louis, MO

car·ni·val [KAHR-nuh-vawl] *noun*

A flesh-eating animal or insectivorous plant.

*"If a flower eats a hot dog then it's a **carnival**."*

—Joseph, age 5, Winnipeg, Canada

cash·er·a·tor [KASH-uhr-ay-tr] *noun*

A business machine that records and regulates business transactions, typically with a cash drawer, number pad, viewscreen, and receipt printer that calculates the total cost of goods sold.

*"The lady puts our money in the **casherator**, and it gives us the change!"*

—Hugo, age 2, Stoney Creek, NC

chap·sticks [CHAHP-stihks] *plural noun*

A pair of thin, tapered sticks typically made of wood, ivory, or plastic that are used as eating utensils by most Asian cultures by holding them between the fingers and thumb of the hand, allowing one to grab food.

*"I can eat with **chapsticks**!"*

—Jada, age 5, Alton, IL

cheese poops [CHEEZ poopz] *collective noun*

Small pieces of puffed corn covered with an orange-yellow cheese-flavored powder that is known to turn anything it comes into contact with the same color.

*"My fingers look like **cheese poops**!"*

—Mallory, age 3, Carrollton, GA

Chick·en Mc·Chung·etts [chihk-en muhk-CHUNG-etz] *plural proper noun*

Small, formed portions of chicken meat, battered and deep-fried, first served by the McDonalds Corporation in 1980, and have since become a favorite food of children around the world.

*"I love to eat **Chicken McChungetts**!"*

—Kane, age 2, Martinsburg, WV

chick·munk [chihk-MUHNGK] *noun*

1. A small, striped, terrestrial squirrel native to North America and Asia.

2. The genus of three fictional performing entertainers who first became famous in the mid-twentieth century.

*"Dad, can the **chickmunk** in our yard play the harmonica too?"*

Also pronounced *chunkmunk*.

—Candice age 2, St. Peters, MO. Additional source: Sophia, age 4, St. Louis, MO

chick·sticks [CHYK-stihks] *plural noun*

Small, rectangular pieces of breaded fish, usually deep-fried or baked and often served with condiments for dipping.

*"We're having **chicksticks** and tarter sauce for lunch!"*

—Madeleine, age 3, Easthampton, MA

chick·en naw·get [CHIK-n NAWG-it] *noun*

A small piece of battered or breaded chicken meat, usually baked or fried, that may also come molded or cut into fun shapes.

*"Cool! This **chicken nawget** looks like a dinosaur!"*

—Jake, age 2, O'Fallon, MO

chick·en pops [CHIHK-ehn poppz] *noun*

An infectious disease, most common in children, caused by the herpes or varicella zoster virus, that causes a mild fever and red, itchy blisters, but afterward leaves the person immune to the disease.

*"You mean I can't get **chicken pops** again?"*

—Alvin, age 5, St. Louis, MO

Chuck·ey·je·sus [chuhk-e-JEE-zuhs] *proper noun*

A restaurant started by Nolan Bushnell in 1977 that caters to children and families by offering animated entertainment, arcade and skill games, indoor rides, food, and party packages for special occasions such as birthdays.

*"I'm going to **Chuckeyjesus** for my birthday!"*

Also pronounced *Chuck Jesus*.

—Max, age 2, St. Louis, MO. Additional source: Josiah, age 4, St. Louis, MO

churts [CHIRTZ] *noun*

A group of people who share the same religious beliefs and worship, commune, and serve in a particular location together that is sometimes referred to by the same name.

*"Our **churts** has puppet shows!"*

Also pronounced *turch*.

—Jessica, age 4, St. Louis, MO. Additional source: Jamie, age 7, Sacramento, CA

cim·ma·nim [SYM-muh-nym] *noun*

An aromatic spice made from the dried and rolled bark of a tree native to Southeast Asia and used to flavor desserts and foods, such as breakfast cereals.

*"I want **cimmanim** in my oatmeal, please!"*

—Lola, age 2, Millersburg, PA

cin·der·el·ish [syn-durh-EHL-ish] *noun*

A condiment of chopped pickles, usually of the sweet variety, used to add flavor to particular foods.

*"I want **cinderelish** on my hot dog!"*

—William, age 4, Bellevue, NE

cir·cus [SIHR-kuhss] *noun*

A complete path that begins and ends in the same place, such as the route electricity follows in an electronic device, which if interrupted, does not allow the device to operate.

*"Dad says he blew a **circus**."*

—Amelia, age 5, Chalmette, LA

clock·ways [KLOHK-wayz] *adverb*

In the same direction of the hands of a clock as viewed straight on, sometimes used for the direction of a sequence of turns in a game.

*"It's my turn now because we're going **clockways**!"*

Also pronounced *clockwards*.

—Mya, age 5, St. Louis, MO

coat·pi·lot [KOHWT-py-loht] *noun*

An aircraft pilot who is second in command, also used sometimes in reference to commandeering other vehicles such as an automobile.

*"Dad, can I be your **coatpilot** on the way to the store?!"*

—Joshua, age 5, St. Louis, MO

col·lege cheese [KOL-lehj CHEEZ] *noun*

A mildly flavored white cheese of semi-solid consistency made from skim milk curds, the process of which will begin if any type of milk sits too long.

*"Eww! That milk looks like **college cheese**!"*

—Kelly, age 3

com·pe·ter [kuhm-PEE-tr] *noun*

An electronic device that processes data at high speeds and stores and retrieves data from itself or external storage devices or through the World Wide Web.

*"I saw pictures of France on our **competer**!"*

—Bennett, age 3, Little Rock, AR

con·fes·sion stand [kuhn-FESH-uhn-stand] *noun*

A structure from which items are sold for consumption, typically at sporting events or amusement parks.

*"Grandma! There's a **confession stand**! Can I get cotton candy?"*

—Mitchell, age 6, St. Louis, MO

con·pus·sion [KUHN-puhsh-shyuhn] *noun*

An injury to the brain or spinal cord, typically from the shock of impact such as a fall or a blow to the head.

*"Dad, Jimmy hit me and gave me a **conpussion!**"*

—Corinne Lily Grace, age 5, Louisville, KY

con·se·ques·tions [KON-si-kwes-tyuhns] *plural noun*

The results, effects, or outcomes of a previous event or series of events, known to be much more severe when forewarned of them by authorities, such as parents or teachers.

*"I listened because Mrs. Grayson told me there would be **consequestions!**"*

—Addison, age 6, St. Louis, MO

con·sti·toot·ed [KOHN-stih-toot-ehd] *adjective*

Slow moving or immobilized due to restriction, such as dehydration or lack of fiber in the bowels.

*"I can't poop because I'm **constitooted!**"*

Also pronounced *concetrated*.

—Megan, age 4, Elgin, OK. Additional source: Audrey, age 4, Sullivan, MO

---

con·struc·tions [kun-STRUHK-shionz] *plural noun*

Ordered information or steps intended to guide in performing an action, completing a task, or assembling an object, such as furniture or machinery, most of which, especially when in written form, have been known to confuse fathers or even cause them to ignore them altogether.

*"It blew up because Dad didn't read the **constructions**."*

Also pronounced *inscructions* and *destructions*.

—Ian, age 5, Rochester, NY. Additional sources: Mary, age 5, Indianapolis, IN; Adric, age 2, Champaign, IL

con·test lens [KOHN-test lehnz] *noun*

A small, plastic disk that holds itself to the cornea of the eye and corrects vision, made clear so as to be unseen, which also makes them difficult to find if they ever fall out.

*"Uh oh! Daddy lost his **contest lens**!"*

—Abby Ann, age 3, Palmdale, CA

cork·n·beans [COURK-n-beens] *noun*

Navy beans cooked with bits of bacon in a sweet, smoky sauce and usually served with barbecue.

*"Grandma is making **cork-n-beans!**"*

—Chad, age 3, Menifee, CA

cou·ple·cake [KUH-puhl-kayk] *noun*

A small, sweetened cake baked in a cup-shaped mold, meant to be individually portioned, but never big enough to satisfy one child.

*"Can I please have another **couplecake?**"*

Also pronounced *pupcake*.

—Cyndi, age 2, St. Louis, MO. Additional sources: Max, age 2, St. Louis, MO; Grant, age 4, Gig Harbor, WA

crab·man·goon [KRAB-man-GOONE] *noun*

A type of Asian dumpling made of wonton wrappers stuffed with cream cheese, crab meat, and seasonings that is deep-fried and served as an appetizer, or a side, but considered by many children to be the main entrée.

"I don't want fried rice, I just want more **crabmangoon!***"*

—Thomas, age 5, Tempe, AZ

crow·bra [KROE-bruh] *noun*

A highly venomous snake of the genera *Naja* or *Ophiophagus* that is native to Africa and characterized by its ability to flatten its neck into hood-like form when threatened.

"I have a book about a spitting **crowbra!***"*

—Caidance, age 3, Tucson, AZ

Crunches

When my brother Alvin had hip surgery years ago, my then five-year-old son, Luke, asked, "Mom, does Uncle Alvin have to walk with crunches now?"

—Olga, Troy, IL

crunch·es [KRUNCH-ez] *plural noun*

A pair of supports that
assist a lame or sick person
in walking, usually with a
crosspiece at one end that
rests under the armpits.

*"Uncle Alvin broke his hip
and has to walk with* **crunches**
now."

—Luke, age 5, St. Louis, MO

crus·tace [KRUS-tess] *noun*

The outer shell or edge formed on baked bread,
pizza, or pies, sometimes disliked by children so
much it is necessary to remove it in its entirety before
consumption.

"Mom, don't forget to tear the **crustace** *off!"*

—Reagan, age 4, St. Louis, MO

cup fold·er [KUHP fohl-dr] *noun*

A device made to hold a drinking vessel upright, often found in vehicles and movie theaters.

*"Look, my seat has a **cup folder**!"*

—Justin, age 3, Langhome, PA

dan·dy·fly·in [DAN-dee-flye-ihn] *noun*

A weed of the daisy family with notched leaves and flowers with edible golden-yellow pedals that are followed by light, hair-like heads with seeds that disperse easily in the wind.

*"Ooh, there's a **dandyflyin**!"*

—Sonorah, age 3, Portland, OR

Dark Vad·er [darhk-VAYE-dr] *proper noun*

A science fiction movie character created by filmmaker George Lucas. The character is noted for his unique outfit that consists of a long black cape and a life-supporting full-body suit, including a helmet with a respirator that emits a unique breathing sound, similar to some real-life devices.

*"Dad, sometimes my humidifier sounds like **Dark Vader.**"*

Also pronounced *Dark Elevator*.

—Zacharey, age 5, Lake Orion, MI. Additional source: Addison, age 4, St. Louis, MO

day·ca·tion [dayh-KAYH-shiun] *noun*

A period of time, usually a week or more and often occurring annually, where work, study, or other normal activity is suspended for rest or recreation, typically away from home.

*"We're going away on **daycation!**"*

—Max, age 3, St. Louis, MO

DBD [dee-bee-DEE] *noun*

An abbreviation for "digital video disc" or "digital versatile disc," which is a thin optical disc capable of storing large amounts of data such as movies, music, images, or text, but will not work if its surface becomes unreadable.

*"Dad, Mikey got peanut butter on my **DBD**!"*

—Sarah, age 4, Seattle, WA

de·fec·tive [dih-FEK-tihv] *noun*

A person, usually a police officer, who investigates criminal activity, obtains information, gathers evidence, or simply recovers lost items around the house.

*"I'm a good **defective** because I found the remote control!"*

—Andy, age 5, Gordon, NSW, Australia

dem·na·strate [DEHM-nuh-strayt] *verb*

To establish, explain, or make evident by means of reason or physical example, such as showing someone how to play a new video game.

*"Allow me to **demnastrate**!"*

—Danny, age 6, Pierre, SD

dia·per·e·na [dye-puhr-EE-nah] *noun*

An intestinal disorder that causes abnormally frequent fecal evacuations, usually with a liquid consistency, but always with a strong smell.

*"Ewww! Becky has **diaperena**!"*

Also pronounced *korea*.

—Gina, age 2, St. Peters, MO. Additional source, Amelia, age 3, Grand Haven, MI

ding·bell [DEENG-behl] *noun*

A bell or chime triggered by a button outside of a door or portal that announces someone's presence.

*"Mom, the **dingbell** is ringing!"*

—Will, age 2, Collinsville, OK; Halina, age 5, San Antonio, TX

dis·cuss·king [diss-KUSS-king] *adjective*

Offensive, sickening, or repulsive in a physical, emotional, moral, or aesthetic way, such as how children feel about healthy foods even if they have never tasted them.

*"Brussels sprouts?!! That's **discussking**!"*

Also pronounced *bistusting*.

—Halina, age 4, San Antonio, TX. Additional source: Kyla, age 3, St. Charles, MO

Dis·kem·ber [diss-KEHM-br] *noun*

The twelfth and last month of the year.

*"Christmas is on **Diskember** 25th!"*

—Cedrick, age 4, Omaha, NE

disk·wash·er [DISK-wahsh-r] *noun*

1. A person who cleans dishes or utensils.

2. A machine that cleans dishes or utensils that can malfunction when loaded with objects not intended for it to clean.

*"I didn't mean to break the **diskwasher**; I just wanted to clean the milk off of my trucks."*

—Timmy, age 6, Birmingham, AL

dis·pend [dihs-PEHND] *verb*

To cease or hold for an indefinite amount of time, such as to be removed from attending school for bad behavior.

*"Will Mr. Clarkson **dispend** me for this?"*

—Britton, age 6, Cranston, RI. Additional source: Mia, age 5, Arlington, VA

dis·tinct [dihs-TINKT] *adjective*
Obsolete or no longer in existence.
*"Dinosaurs are **distinct**."*

—Jasmin, age 9, Alton, IL

down·chairs [DOUN-chairz] *adjective, adverb, noun*
A lower floor of a structure or building, or the
direction thereof.
*"Dad, the dog pooped **downchairs**!"*
See also *upchairs*.

—Jessica, age 3, St. Louis, MO

dy·nam·i·cal [dye-NAM-ih-kuhl] *adjective*
Connecting two opposing corners of any straight-
sided shape, such as from the bottom left of a square
to its top right.
*"Mom cuts my toast **dynamical**."*

—Melissa, age 5, Lowell, MI

ear·ding [EER-deeng] *noun*

An ornament or piece of jewelry that is worn on the earlobe or other part of the ear.

*"Mom, my **earding** fell out!"*

—Bridgette, age 2, Auburn, IN

ear·plums [EER-pluhmz] *plural noun*

A pair of soft, pliable pieces of material that are inserted into the openings of the ears to protect them from water or sound, such as children playing in the afternoon.

*"Mom can't take a nap without her **earplums**!"*

—Brendon, age 4, Fort Collins, CO

ears·drop·ping [EERS-drop-eeng] *verb*

To listen in on a conversation that was intended to be private.

*"Daddy! Jimmy was **earsdropping** on us again!"*

—Ronesha, St. Louis, MO

earth·qua·tor [URTH-kwey-tur] *noun*

A line of measurement that spans the earth, perpendicular to its axis, at equal distance from both poles and closest to the Sun, making it the hottest area on the surface of the planet.

*"It's as hot as the **earthquator** out there!"*

—Enna, age 6, Tallahassee, FL

eff·el·ent [EF-ehl-ent] *noun*

A large, grayish-brown, five-toed animal with a long, hose-like nose and large ears, which is the largest animal on land.

*"I saw an **effelent** at the zoo today!"*

Also pronounced *effanent*, *ellament*, and *pellypunt*.

—Julia, age 4, St. Louis, MO. Additional sources: Madison, age 2, St. Charles, MO; Emily, age 2, Colville, WA; Pam, age 4, Crestview, FL

el·bone [EHL-bowhn] *noun*

The joint of the human arm between the forearm and the upper arm.

*"Ouch! I hit my **elbone**!"*

Also pronounced *elmo.*

—Bridgette, age 3, Auburn, IN. Additional source: Thomas, age 2, Louisville, KY

ell·e·gat·or [EL-uh-gay-ter] *noun*

A vertically moving cabin, cage, or platform in a structure or building that moves people or freight from one level to another.

*"Mommy! Let's ride the **ellegator**!"*

—Gabi, age 3, MO

em·mi·ni·tion [ehm-mih-NISH-uhn] *noun*

A supply of material that is detonated from, dropped out of, or fired from a weapon, such as foam darts from a toy gun.

*"Time out, guys! I'm out of **emminition**!"*

—Addison, age 7, St. Louis, MO

er·rupt·ing [ihr-RUHPT-eeng] *verb*

The act of breaking the continuity or course of something, such as to speak while someone else is already speaking.

"Mom! Bobby keeps errupting me!"

—Ben, age 4, Tallahassee, FL

ex·pla·na·tion point [eks-pluh-NAY-shun poynt] *noun*

The punctuation mark (!) used in writing to convey intensity, emotion, or loudness.

"An explanation point means you're yelling!"

Also pronounced *estimation point.*

—Kendra, age 6, Lawton, OK. Additional source: Garrett, age 3

ex·ski·ted [ecks-SKYE-tehd] *adjective*

Emotionally stimulated, such as when awaiting the arrival of an anticipated activity or event.

"Dad, I'm exskited to go to the beach tomorrow!"

Also pronounced *skited.*

—Stan, age 3, Jacksonville, FL. Additional source: Jack, age 2, Indianapolis, IN

ex·tra·size [EKS-truh-sahyz] *verb*

To engage in a physical activity for the sake of training the body or improving health and fitness, such as walking or running.

*"Gym class gives me good **extrasize!**"*

—Gage, age 3, Paradis, LA. Additional source: Lucy, age 4, St. Louis, MO

eye·shal·low [EHYE-shahl-loe] *noun*

A colored and sometimes glittery or reflective cosmetic powder that is applied to the eyelids and the skin around the eye for emphasis.

*"Mom looks pretty with **eyeshallow!**"*

—Bekkah, age 5, Los Angeles, CA

eye·stache [AHY-stash] *noun*

A short, thick, curved hair that grows on the fringe of the upper and lower eyelids to protect the eyes and that fall out every 150 to 200 days allowing a new one to grow in its place.

*"I found an **eyestache** on my shirt today!"*

—Benedicte, age 3, Washington, D.C.

---

fab·li·ous [FAB-lee-uhs] *adjective*

Exceptionally or incredibly good, pleasing, or successful.

*"Your picture looks **fablious**!"*

—Addison, age 6, St. Louis, MO

far·mer·john [FAR-mur-jon] *noun*

A hard, dry Italian skim milk cheese usually grated and served atop foods such as a salad or baked meal.

*"I want more **farmerjohn** on my pizza, please!"*

—Original source unknown

Feb·nu·ar·y [FEHB-new-ayr-ee] *noun*

The second and shortest month of the year, normally consisting of 28 days, but is 29 days long during leap years.

*"There's no **Febnuary** 29th this year?"*

Also pronounced *Fibrillary.*

—Justin, age 5, Freemont, NE. Additional source: Karen, age 4, Clarksville, TN

fight·er-fight·er [FYE-ter-FYE-ter] *noun*

A person who exterminates or contains fires, and often rescues people and animals endangered by the flames. The occupation is among the top vocational choices of all children.

*"When I grow up I'm gonna be a **fighter-fighter**, too!"*

—Jaedon, age 4, Wichita, KS

fi·ren [FYE-rehn] *noun*

An acoustical device that produces and projects loud sounds as a warning, such as on a fire engine.

*"I hear a **firen** coming, Daddy!"*

—Eleanor, age 3, St. Louis, MO

flock·a·ming·o [FLOHK-uh-meen-goh] *noun*

An aquatic bird of the *Phoenicopteridae* family, with long, thin legs, a long neck, and a downward pointed bill best known for its pink color that is so beautiful it has often inspired people in American culture to use its likeness as a lawn decoration.

"Mom, how come Grandma's flockamingo never moves?"

Also pronounced *ingo ingo*.

—Emily, age 4, St. Peters, MO. Additional source: Naomi, age 2, Iowa City, IA

floss teeth [FLOHSS teehth] *collective noun*

Removable artificial teeth; dentures.

"Grandma's floss teeth fell out!"

—Emma, age 5, Springfield, MO

flus·ter·at·ed [FLUSS-tur-ay-ted] *adjective*

Feeling disappointment or aggravation by a situation or circumstance.

*"That makes me very **flusterated**!"*

—Justin, age 5, Saint John, New Brunswick, Canada

flut·ter·by [FLUH-tuhr-bye] *noun*

An insect of the *Lepidoptera* order, characterized by a thin body and large, broad wings that are usually quite colorful.

*"Ooh! Look at that pretty **flutterby**!"*

—Erik, age 2, Moro, IL. Additional source: Kaydence, age 3, Rolling Hills, WY

food·ger·a·tor [FOOD-jur-ay-tur] *noun*

A household appliance in which perishable foods are kept cool by means of mechanical cooling, the outside of which has become the most common location for displaying children's artistic creations.

*"Mom put my pirate ship on the **foodgerator**!"*

Also pronounced *fridgeator, fridgaracer*, and *freridgerator*.

—Colin, age 3, Vermilion, OH. Additional sources: Adam, age 4, Alvin, TX; Emma, age 4, Ste. Genevieve, MO; Travis, age 5, Moran, KS; David, age 5, St. Louis, MO

for·ne·ver [fohr-NEH-vr] adverb

Without end, continually, such as how long any undesirable event feels to a child.

*"This is taking **fornever**!"*

—Timmy, age 6, O'Fallon, MO

frap·pas·ti·no [frap-pahs-TEE-no] *proper noun*

A brand name registered and trademarked by the Starbuck's Corporation for their own line of espresso-based iced coffee drinks.

*"My Daddy buys a big **frappastino** every morning!"*

—Samantha Laine, age 4, Brooklyn, NY

Fri·der·day [FRYE-dur-daye] *proper noun*

The sixth day of the week, before Saturday and after Thursday. It is typically the most popular weekday among children because it initiates the weekend, when there is no school.

*"Yay! It's **Friderday**!"*

—Drew, age 3, St. Louis, MO

fruit cot・ton・tail [froot COHT-tun-tayle] *noun*

A serving of mixed fruit slices or pieces that is offered as an appetizer or dessert.

*"When I'm done eating, can I have a **fruit cottontail?**"*

—Elizabeth, age 4, St. Louis, MO. Additional source: Nichole, age 3, Albuquerque, NM

fu・ton [FOO-tawn] *noun*

A small piece of baked, toasted, or fried seasoned bread, used as a garnish for salads, soups, or just as a snack.

*"Mom, can I have another **futon?**"*

Also pronounced *tooton*.

—Nathan, age 3, Valdosta, GA. Additional source: Dylan, age 3, Charlotte, NC

If It Ain't Fixed . . .

One night when my son Tim was five, we noticed our dog was limping really bad and seemed to be in a lot of pain. We took him to an animal hospital and when the nurse at the front desk asked us if he was "fixed," before I could answer my son blurted out, "No ma'am, he's broke! That's why we're here."

—Allie, Raleigh, NC

gam·pire [GHAM-pyre] *noun*

A mythical creature that reanimates at night for fear of sunlight and sustains itself from the blood of living beings, preferably humans.

*"Mom, lock my window tonight so a **gampire** doesn't get in and bite me!"*

—Aiden, age 5, Fenton, MO

gem·nu·ine [JEHM-nyew-ihn] *adjective*

Absolutely authentic and true, such as a rare, precious stone.

*"You mean it's a real **gemnuine** diamond?"*

—Emily, age 4, Brookside, DE

ge·zaust·ed [GEH-zaws-ted] *adjective*

Drained of physical or mental resources, such as when tired after a long day of activity.

*"I'm **gezausted** from school!"*

—Hannah, age 3, Rohnert Park, CA

ghost cheese [GOHWST cheez] *noun*

A cheese made from goat's milk, typically with a stronger flavor than cheeses from cow's milk, making it difficult for some children to adjust to.

*"But I don't like **ghost cheese** because it tastes funny!"*

—Libby, age 5, Lee's Summit, MO

girl cheese [GURHL cheez] *noun*

A hot sandwich typically made with a slice of American, Swiss, or cheddar cheese placed between two slices of buttered bread and grilled.

*"Mom, can I have a **girl cheese** with my tomato soup?"*

—Brad, age 3, Bothell, WA

glass·a·ble [GLASS-ah-bl] *adjective*

Able to be easily broken, such as something made of a fragile material.

*"Be careful, that's **glassable**!"*

—Leah, age 2, Kansas City, MO

glass·hum·per [GLASS-hum-pr] *noun*

A plant-eating insect of the family *Acrididae*, common to grassy places, with long hind legs used for jumping and for producing a chirping sound, typically at night.

"Mom, I can hear a **glasshumper** *outside my window!"*

—Perry, age 4, Milwaukee, WI

glit·ter·bug [GLIT-tr-buhgg] *noun*

A person who throws their refuse in a public place rather than a waste recepticle.

"I'm not a **glitterbug** *because I use the trash can!"*

—Nancy, age 4, Newport, RI

go·nut [GOE-nuht] *noun*

Fried sweetened dough, usually round with a hole in the middle, that is sometimes glazed with sweet icing and even topped with candy decorations.

*"Can I have a **gonut** with sprinkles on it?"*

Also pronounced *dognut.*

—Tabitha, age 4, Little Rock, AR. Additional source: Unknown, age 3, Richmond Hill, Ontario, Canada

Getting Bigger

One day when my three-year-old daughter, Ellie, was with her Grandma, she asked for candy but was instead offered an apple. Ellie was not interested in this, but my mother-in-law told her that not only was an apple better for her than candy, but it would also make her bigger. This interested Ellie, as she is the youngest of our three children and eager to catch up in size. So she happily ate the apple and then began looking herself over, inspecting her arms and legs, and then finally looked up and said, "Nana, I'm not big yet!"

—Margaret, St. Louis, MO

go·rill·a bar [guh-RILL-uh bahr] *noun*

A thin, typically rectangular cookie made from a mixture of rolled oats, brown sugar or honey, dried fruit, and nuts.

*"Mom, can I have a **gorilla bar** for my snack?"*

—Saylor, age 3, OH

gods·ball [GODZ-bawl] *noun*

A group game in which players try to eliminate their opponents by hitting each other with a semi-soft inflated ball. The last remaining unhit person is the winner.

*"We played **godsball** in gym today and I won!"*

—Mya, age 5, Ferguson, MO

Gon·zil·la [gohn-zihl-lah] *proper noun*

A fictional giant Japanese monster, first appearing in Ishiro Honda's 1954 film *Gojira* and has since become a pop icon as well as a reference for something monstrous, such as an appetite.

*"Mom says I eat like **Gonzilla!**"*

—Timothy, age 4, Greenville, IN

grad·i·ate [GRAJ-ee-ayt] *verb*

To complete a course of study, which is commemorated by a ceremony where one is presented with a degree or diploma from the educational institution.

*"When I finish school I can **gradiate!**"*

—Anthony, age 6, Albany, GA

Great Nuts [GRAYT nuhtz] *proper noun*

A brand-named cereal of natural wheat and barley, first created in 1897 by C.W. Post, typically served for breakfast.

*"Dad, I want **Great Nuts** with sugar, please!"*

Also pronounced *graymupps*.

—Stanley, age 4, Flagstaff, NM. Additional source: Gabriel, age 4, Carrollton, TX

guy·jan·tic [gye-JAHN-tic] *adjective*

Very large in size, such as a giant or a very tall structure.

*"The Empire State Building is **guyjantic!**"*

—Kendra, age 3, Las Cruces, NM

gy·ro·phone [JYE-rowe-fohne] *noun*

A musical instrument of graduating suspended wooden bars arranged in the same manner as a piano keyboard, which is played by striking the bars with small wooden or plastic mallets.

*"I want to play a **gyrophone**!"*

—Oliver, age 3, Binghamton, NY

gym·ma·gics [jim-MAA-jiks] *noun*

The art or competitive sport of physical feats of exercise such as jumping, swinging, balancing, or any combination thereof.

*"I did a cartwheel on the big bar in **gymmagics** today!"*

—Emma, age 4, Kingsland, GA

gym·sta·di·um [jihm-STAYE-dee-uhm] *noun*

A large indoor area for sporting activities or gymnastics, such as for a physical education class. The area also can be used to host other large gatherings such as an assembly.

*"The whole school was in the **gymstadium** today!"*

—Madison, age 6, Anoka, MN

Hair·y Pot·ty [HAYR-ee POHT-tee] *proper noun*

The main character in the fantasy book series by British author J.K. Rowling. He is a young orphaned boy who discovers he has magical powers, and he is characterized by dark hair, a small lightning-shaped scar on his forehead, and unique, black round-rimmed glasses.

"Look Dad, that kid looks like ***Hairy Potty****!"*

—Jakob, age 5, Florissant, MO

64   Alvin Zamudio

han·dy·camp [HAN-dee-kamp] *noun*

A physical or mental disability that limits someone from performing normal tasks such as walking long distances at places of business.

*"Don't park there because that's a **handycamp** spot!"*

—Stevie, age 4, St. Louis, MO

han·gub·ber [HAN-guh-br] *noun*

A fried or grilled beef patty, usually served on a bread bun.

*"I want a **hangubber** and French fries!"*

Also pronounced *hagenberger, hambugger, hangermer,* or *cheekaburger.*

—Christopher, Omaha, NE. Additional sources: Kirsta, age 4, Ferguson, MO; Ashley, age 8, St. Charles, MO

han·i·ti·zer [HAN-ih-tye-zr] *noun*

An antiseptic gel, foam, or other liquid used on the hands to make them clean and hygenic.

*"I use **hanitizer** after I wash my hands!"*

—Hailey, age 3, Columbia, IL. Additional sources: Chloie, age 3, Council Bluffs, IA; Kira, age 6, Flagstaff, AZ

Har·mon·i·ca [hahr-MON-ih-kah] *proper noun*

An eight-day-long Jewish holiday that commemorates the rededication of the Temple in Jerusalem in 165 BC, which begin on the 25th day of Kislev and is symbolized by the daily lighting of eight candles.

*"Dad, if we celebrate **Harmonica** do we get more presents?"*

—Olivia, age 6, Otsego, MN

hash·brow [hash-brou] *noun*

The ridge above the eye, or the hair growing on it, which sometimes gets bushier as one gets older.

*"Daddy, your **hashbrow** itches me when I give you hugs!"*

—Caidance, age 3, Tucson, AZ

heart · beep [HART-beep] *noun*

A complete pulsation of the heart that can be heard by a stethoscope or by simply laying your head on another's chest.

*"Mom, I can hear your **heartbeep**!"*

—Sophie, age 3, Geneva, NY

hic · cup truck [HIHK-uhp truhk] *noun*

A vehicle with a small cab and a larger rear bed made for carrying goods and materials, such as wood, stone, animals, or people.

*"Dad, can we ride in the back of your **hiccup truck**?"*

—Max, age 2, Ann Arbor, MI

hip·po·bot·tom·less [hipp-oh-BOTT-uhm-lehss] *noun*

A large plant-eating amphibious mammal native to Africa, with a thick hairless body, short legs, a large head, and a wide-mouthed muzzle.

*"If we go to the zoo, can I see a **hippobottomless?**"*

Also pronounced *hippopamanus*.

—Alex, age 7, St. Louis, MO. Additional source: Emily, age 3, Rochester, NY

Ho·ly Spear·mint [hoh-lee SPEER-mint] *proper noun*

The third person of the Holy Trinity in Christian theology, believed to be the manifest presence of and the power of God.

*"In the name of the Father, the Son, and the **Holy Spearmint!**"*

—Cade, age 3, Hammond, LA

Holy Humor

I once overheard a young boy in church praying, "Our Father who art in Heaven, Howard be thy name . . ." I almost passed out trying to keep from busting out laughing!

—Marianne, Sacramento, CA

---

hon·ey·bird [HUHN-ee-byrd] *noun*

A small, nectar-sipping bird of the *Trochilidae* family, characterized by its colorful iridescent plumage, its slender bill, and its ability to hover and fly backward.

*"Look Mom, there's a **honeybird**!"*

Also pronounced *dummybird*.

—Thomas, age 4, Loganville, WI. Additional source: Casey, age 5, Flagstaff, AZ

hook·ups [HOOHK-uhps] *noun*

A temporary disorder in which the diaphragm spasms involuntarily, forcing quick bursts of inhalation and a sudden closure of the glottis, which produces a sound like a short, sharp cough.

*"Bobby has the **hookups**!"*

—Isaac, age 4, St. Louis, MO

hop·pi·cop·per [HOP-pee-kop-per] *noun*

An aircraft without wings, lifted by a series of rotating overhead blades.

"Look, there's a **hoppicopper!***"*

Also pronounced *hoppercopper, hopcopper, hottopotter, hot-topter, celihopter,* and *hoptractor.*

—Christopher, age 4, Colorado Springs, CO. Additional sources: Caleb, age 4, Grand Prairie, TX; Jonathan, age 2, Olathe, KS; Alix, age 2, St. Louis, MO; Kyle, age 3, Alton, IL

horn [hohrn] *noun*

A sharp extension on the stem of a plant that can poke your finger.

"I gotta be careful! That flower has **horns** *on it!"*

—Connor, age 2, Ferguson, MO

hos·ti·pull [HOHS-tih-pool] *noun*

A facility where people go when they are sick or injured. It is a place where doctors and nurses do things to you that may hurt at the time but help you feel better afterward.

*"Do I have to go to the **hostipull**, Dad?"*

Also pronounced *hospible*, *hawsabibble*, and *hostible*.

—Julia and Veronica, age 4, St. Louis, MO. Additional sources: Chad, age 3, Menifee, CA; Claire, age 4, Cedar Park, TX; unknown, age 5, Hazelwood, MO

hu·man·fire [HUE-mahn-fyre] *noun*

A device that vaporizes water to increase or maintain a moisture level in the atmosphere of a room.

*"Mom, you need to put more water in the **humanfire**."*

—Kyle, age 2, St. Louis, MO

hunk·ar·a·zun·kle [huhnk-uhr-uh-ZUHN-kl] *adjective*

Flat, parallel, or level to the horizon and at a right angle to vertical.

*"When I sleep I lay **hunkarazunkle**!"*

—Art, age 5, St. Louis, MO

hy·po·glyph·ics [hye-poe-GLIF-ihks]
collective noun

An ancient written script in which pictorial symbols
represent phrases, words, or meanings.

*"Egyptians used **hypoglyphics**."*

—Addison, age 7, St. Louis, MO

ice crime [AIYSS-kryme] *noun*

A frozen dessert made with
sweetened milk, cream,
butterfat, and other
flavorings, typically served
in an edible cone or a bowl.

*"We're having cake and **ice
crime** for my birthday!"*

—Abriella, age 2, Mason, OH

il·lus·tri·ci·ty [ihl-luhs-TRIH-sih-tee] *noun*

A form of energy that utilizes charged particles as a current that travels through a conductible material, usually copper wire, enabling any manner of devices to operate when connected to it, such as a home entertainment system.

*"We can't watch movies right now because the **illustricity** went out!"*

—Jacob, age 4, Blackfoot, ID

im·pla·ma·tion [im-pluh-MEY-shun] *noun*

Knowledge acquired through experience, discussion, study, research, or instruction.

*"Sorry Mom, but I need more **implamation**."*

—Mya, age 5, St. Louis, MO

in·car·pe·ter [ihn-KAHR-peh-tr] *noun*

A person who translates writing or speech from one language into another, such as from English to Spanish.

*"Juan needs an **incarpeter**!"*

—Olivia, age 4, Billings, MT

in·sect fin·ger [IHN-sekt feen-guhr] *noun*

The first finger on the hand, next to the thumb.

*"I point with my **insect finger**!"*

—Penelope, age 3, West Hartford, CT

in·struc·tion pa·per [in-STRUHK-shion pay-pr] *noun*

A heavyweight paper that comes in various colors that is primarily used for cutting out shapes, making posters, or other items.

*"I made a hat out of **instruction paper**!"*

—Mya, age 5, St. Louis, MO

ja·ma·mas [juh-MAH-muhz] *plural noun*

Lightweight clothing worn for sleeping, sometimes colored and decorated with images of storybook characters.

*"I sleep in fairy princess **jamamas**!"*

Also pronounced *kajama*.

—Lily, age 2, Colorado Springs, CO. Additional source: Kaitlyn, age 3, San Diego, CA

jag·roar [JAHG-rowr] *noun, proper noun*

1. A large cat, native to the forests of Central and South America, with a golden coat and black spots.

2. A very expensive car.

*"Dr. Kimball drives a **Jagroar!**"*

—Jimmy, age 4, Fargo, ND

Je·sus crack·er [JEE-zuhs krahk-r] *noun*

A small, square, brand-named cheddar-cheese flavored biscuit, baked thin and crisp and favored by children since its invention in 1921 by Green & Green Company of Dayton, OH.

*"Can I have another **Jesus cracker**, please?"*

—Carter, age 3, Colorado Springs, CO

It's All in the Name

One Sunday in children's church when they were talking about calling out Jesus's name when you need help, I overheard a child say proudly, "My Dad knows all about that because he yells for 'Jesus Christ' all the time when he's fixing stuff!"

—Stew, Baton Rouge, LA

jug·gle·man [JUHG-gl-muhn] *noun*

A civilized man of good background, breeding, education, and social stature, such as a man who opens a door for a lady.

*"Dad, you're a real **juggleman!**"*

—Bella, age 2, Gardner, KS

jump·ing·bean [juhmp-eeng-BEEN] *noun*

A stretching, resilient canvas attached by several equally spaced springs to a supporting horizontal frame, used for jumping or other acrobatic or gymnastic exercises.

*"Mom, can I go bounce on the **jumpingbean?**"*

—Melissa, Marysville, WA

kan·ga·roof [kain-gah-RUFE] *noun*

A fur-covered, undomesticated marsupial native to the continent of Australia with short forelimbs, powerful hind limbs that they leap with, a small head, and a large tail.

*"Dad, can we get a **kangaroof** for my birthday?"*

—Alana, age 2, Mexico

key·weed [KEE-weehd] *noun*

A small fruit of the Chinese gooseberry plant characterized by a bright green, sweet, and tangy flesh with dark edible seeds. The fruit is covered by an edible thin hairy brownish skin that is high in antioxidants, but usually does not appeal to children's fickle tastes.

*"Mom, can you peel a **keyweed** for me?"*

—James, age 4, Cape Girardeau, MO

ko·key·o·key [koh-kee-OH-kee] *noun*

A social activity in which people sing popular songs with the backing track. The original vocals have been removed, which often means the performance is nowhere close to the quality of the original.

*"Grandma is terrible at **kokeyokey**!"*

—Jesse, age 3, El Sobrante, CA

kock·u·la·tor [KOK-you-lay-tuhr] *noun*

An electronic device used to perform various mathematical functions but is most popular with younger children for its many enduring buttons.

*"Dad, I think I broke your **kockulator**."*

Also pronounced *calcaputer*.

—Harry, age 5, Keene, NH. Additional source: Candice, age 2, St. Peters, MO

lab·ra·dor re·cei·ver [LAHB-ruh-door re-SEE-vehr] *noun*

A breed of dog originally from Newfoundland, with a short, thick, black, brown, or yellow coat, known for its insatiable desire to chase after and return anything you throw.

*"Dad, can we get a **labrador receiver**?"*

—Andrew, age 4, Salem, IL

land·scrap·er [LAHND-skray-pr] *noun*

A person who improves or maintains the aesthetic appearance of land, such as adding plants and trees or creating a stone pathway.

*"Dad hired a **landscraper** to do the yard!"*

—Nikki, age 6, Raleigh, NC

las·ter·day [LAS-tur-daye] *noun*

The day preceding the current day, or for many children any day before the current day.

*"But Mom, I just cleaned my room **lasterday!**"*

Also pronounced *last-day.*

—Hayden, age 2, Littleton, CO. Additional source: Jackson, age 3, O'Fallon, MO

last·er·night [LAST-uhr-nyte] *noun*

The night preceding the current day or night.

*"But Dad, we brushed our teeth **lasternight!**"*

—Regan, age 2, Jacksonville, FL. Additional source: Sammy Joe, age 3, Kalamazoo, MI

lel·low [LEL-oh] *noun*

A color of the rainbow between orange and green. Also the color of lemons and egg yolks.

*"Dad, why is pee **lellow?**"*

Also pronounced *wellow.*

—Addison, age 3, St. Louis, MO. Additional source: Gabriel, age 4, Scott AFB, IL

lem·on·time [LEHM-uhn-tyme] *noun*

A small variety of tangerine grown in the Mediterranean regions and North and South Africa, with a sweet taste and deep orange-red skin.

*"Mom, can you please peel me a **lemontime?**"*

—Ian, age 3, Richmond, VA

lem·on·zine [lehm-uhn-ZEEN] *noun*

An automobile, usually a standard sedan or SUV, in which the rear passenger section is lengthened, allowing it to accomodate more passengers or to create a more spacious and enhanced interior for luxury transport.

*"Dad, can we get a **lemonzine?**"*

—Jackie, age 5, Boulder, CO

lie·berr·y [LAHY-behr-ee] *verb*

A room or facility that stores books or other media for on-site use or lending for short periods of time.

*"Mom, I got a book from the **lieberry** today!"*

Also pronounced *lyberry* and *whyworry*.

—Addison, St. Louis, MO. Additional sources: Cole, age 3, SC; Gretchen, age 2, MO

light bolt [LYTE bowlt] *noun*

A glass bulb with a metal base inserted into an electrical socket that emits light when electric current passes through its interior, which is typically an inert gas or a light-emitting filament in a vacuum.

*"Dad, the **light bolt** went out in my room!"*

—Bennett, age 4, Little Rock, AK

lip·stache [LIHP-stash] *noun*

Unshaven hair grown on the upper lip. Although it is thickest and most common on men, it is occasionally visible on older women.

*"Dad, Grandma has a **lipstache**!"*

—Cordelia, age 5, Nashville, IN

lip·stitch [LIHP-stihch] *noun*

A tubular-shaped oil- or wax-based cosmetic used to color the lips. It also has been known to serve other purposes such as a medium for children's wall art.

*"Look Mommy! I can draw with **lipstitch**!"*

Also pronounced *lip claws*.

—Kristin, age 4, Chesterfield, MO. Additional source: Mya, age 5, St. Louis, MO

liv·er room [LIHV-er roohm] *noun*

A room in a home typically used for family activities such as entertaining guests, watching television, or imaginary outings.

*"Can we camp out in the **liver room** tonight?"*

—Benjamin, age 2, Clarendon, TX

lock·ie-talk·ie [LOHK-ee-TAHLK-ee] *noun*

A portable electronic device that both receives and transmits audio signal, used for all manner of two-way communication, such as by the military or the police.

*"He called for backup on his **lockie-talkie**!"*

—Sean, age 3, Colorado Springs, CO

---

lump·ster [LUMPS-tr] *noun, plural*

A crustacean (shellfish) with big claws that big people like to eat.

*"Mom and Dad went out to eat some **lumpster**!"*

—Unknown, Cape Coral/Fort Myers, FL

Lunk·y Charms [LUNK-ee chahrmz] *plural noun*

A name-brand breakfast cereal first introduced in 1964 and made from toasted oat pieces and multi-colored, sweetened marshmallow bits, the latter of which tend to dissappear faster when in the hands of unsupervised children.

*"Mom, Ellie ate all the marshmallows in the **Lunky Charms**!"*

—Mya, age 5, St. Louis, MO

ma·chos [MAH-chohz] *collective noun*

A traditional Mexican food consisting of a plate or basket of fried tortilla chips topped with grated or crumbled cheese and sometimes other toppings, such as seasoned meat, refried beans, or peppers, that is baked or broiled.

*"I love hot **machos!**"*

—Dylan, age 3, St. Louis, MO

mag·a·na·zine [mahg-ah-nah-ZEEN] *noun*

A bound paper publication issued periodically, typically full color and containing articles and photographs specializing in specific aspects of culture, such as home improvement or the latest fashion trends.

*"I saw it in a **maganazine!**"*

—Sheila, age 5, Beaverton, OR. Additional source: Ben, age 4, Toledo, OH

Ma·gic·ass·car [ma-jik-ASS-kahr] *proper noun*

1. An island in the Indian Ocean off the southeast coast of Africa, colonized by France.

2. A popular children's movie named after the same island, where the end of the movie takes place.

"Can we watch **Magicasscar** *again?"*

—Jessie, age 3, St. Charles, MO

mag·na·fly·ing glass [MAG-nuh-flyh-eeng glahss] *noun*

A handheld lens that enlarges the image of any object seen through it, such as an ant or a splinter in one's finger.

"You can't see it without a **magnaflying glass***!"*

—Alora, age 5, Asheville, NC

mack·a·mo·ley [makk-uh-MOH-lee] *noun*

A traditional Mexican dish of mashed avocadoes mixed with tomatoes, onions, and seasonings that has a greenish-brown color, typically served as a condiment or dip.

"Mom made **mackamoley** *and chips!"*

—Greger, age 3, Dublin, OH

make·be·lief [MAYK-beh-leef] *noun*

The leaf of the maple tree.

*"Look Dad, a **makebelief**!"*

—Harold, age 3, St. Louis, MO

malls·ber·ry [MAHLZ-beyr-ree] *noun*

A dark red, semi-sweet fruit of a tree or bush that is native to the Far East but has been cultivated in other countries and regions.

*"Look Mommy, there's a **mallsberry** bush."*

Also pronounced *maltberry*.

—Stephanie, age 4, Gary, IN. Additional source: Jamie, age 3, Harlingen, TX

Mal·wart [MAHL-warht] *proper noun*

A retail store chain started in 1962 by Sam Walton whose strategy for higher sales through lower prices has made the franchise international as well as a household name.

*"I got it at **Malwart**."*

—Jill, age 4, O'Fallon, MO

man·eggs [MANN-eyhgz] *noun*

A dressing made from egg yolks, oil, vinegar, or lemon juice and other seasonings used in salads or vegetable dishes or as a condiment for sandwiches.

"Grandma, can you make my baloney sandwich with **maneggs?***"*

Also pronounced *mandaze*.

—Kathryn, age 3, Edwardsville, IL. Additional source: Robert, age 4, Belleville, IL

man·i·mal [MANN-ih-mahl] *noun*

Any multicellular organism with a defined form, sensory and nervous systems, and an ability to voluntarily acquire and internally digest its own food.

"A cow is a **manimal!***"*

Also pronounced *amanimal*, *anaminamal*, and *anamammal*.

—Jackie age 4, Columbus, OH. Additional sources: Teddy, age 3, Jackson, MS; Emily, age 3, Willis, TX; Molly, age 3, Galveston, TX

Man·y·nems [MENN-ee-nemz] *proper noun*

A world-famous confection of milk chocolate with a hard-candy shell that may not melt in your hands but will certainly have disastrous results if left in children's pockets for long periods of time.

*"Mommy, can I have some more **Manynems**? Mine are all melted!"*

Also pronounced *Nim-Nims*.

—Christopher age 2, Colorado Springs, CO. Additional source: Tala, age 3, Belleville, IL

Mar·tin Liv·er King Jr. *proper noun*

An American clergyman, activist, and prominent leader in the African-American civil rights movement who was assassinated in 1968.

—Andrew, age 6, St. Louis, MO

Ma·ry Puf·fins [mah-ree PUHF-finz] *proper noun*

The main character in a series of children's books written by P. L. Travers beginning in 1934. The character is a magical English nanny who flies with her umbrella, a feat most parents fear their children will attempt at some point in their lives.

*"Look Mom, I'm **Mary Puffins**!"*

—Jonah, age 5, Midlothian, VA

mau·mow·er [MAW-mohw-r] *noun*

A machine, hand-pushed or ridden, for cutting grass, often very loudly.

*"I can't hear you because Dad's using the **maumower**!"*

Also pronounced *elmer*.

—Ryan, age 1, Cheyenne, WY. Additional sources: Michelle & Levi, age 2, St. Louis, MO

---

me·ga·dent [MEH-guh-dehnt] *noun*

Any piece of iron or steel with the ability to attract and attach itself other metals or objects with metal surfaces, such as a refrigerator.

*"Look Mom, the **megadent** holds my picture up!"*

Also pronounced *magneck*.

—Jasmin, age 3, Alton, IL. Additional source: Max, age 3, St. Louis, MO

Mel·mo [MEHL-moh] *proper noun*

A beloved children's television show puppet that is a furry red monster with large, white eyes, an orange nose, and a squeaky voice.

*"I love **Melmo**!"*

—Malachi, age 2, Madison, WI

mem·bo·ry card [MEM-boh-ree KAHRD] *noun*

A small removable device with an electronic chip that is used in electronic devices for storing and retrieving data, such as the last level played in a video game.

*"I'm coming Dad, I'm just waiting for the **membory card** to save my game!"*

—Addison, age 6, St. Louis, MO

me·mi·psy·cho [MEM-ee-sye-koh] *noun*

A two-wheeled motorized vehicle, similar to but typically larger than a bicycle, known among children for its ability to give its owner a higher social status.

*"My Dad is awesome because he has a **memipsycho**!"*

Also pronounced *motorcircle.*

—Donna, age 3, St. Louis, MO. Additional source: Noah, age 3, St. Cloud, MN

me·ni·corn [MEH-nih-korn] *noun*

A mythical creature with the body and head of a horse characterized by a single spiraled horn protruding from its forehead.

*"I wish I could ride a real **menicorn**."*

—Cory, age 3, St. Peters, MO

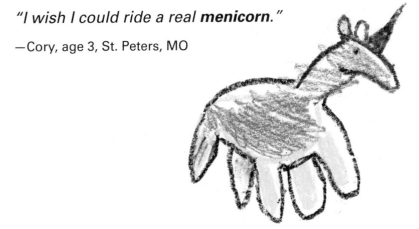

mer·ma·naid

[MEHR-muh-nayd] *noun*

A mythical creature of the sea with the head, arms, and torso of a woman and the tail of a fish.

"She swims like a mermanaid!"

—Lilly, age 3, Charlotte, NC

mes·sin·mess [mehss-ihn MEHSS] *noun*

An abbreviation for short message (or messaging) service that enables cellular phones to transmit and receive alphanumeric text messages of up to 160 characters.

*"Mom, does your phone have **messinmess?**"*

—Alethia, age 3, Indonesia

mik·end·wave [MAHYK-ahnd-wayve] *noun*

An oven that uses electromagnetic waves to heat and cook food.

"Mom, can you make some popcorn in the mikendwave?"

—Robby, age 4, Princeton, NJ

min·der [MAHYN-dr] *noun*

A person who works under the surface of the earth to extract minerals or metallic ore.

*"I want to be a gold **minder**!"*

—Addison, age 6, St. Louis, MO

Min·i·ap·ple·sauce [minn-ee-AP-puhl-sohss] *proper noun*

A city in southeast Minnesota, on the Mississippi River.

*"My Uncle David lives in **Miniapplesauce**."*

—Ignatius, age 3, Toledo, OH

Mis·ter·sip·pi [mis-tuhr-SIP-ee] *proper noun*

1. A state in the southern United States, established in 1817.

2. A primary U.S. river that flows south from the state of Minnesota to the Gulf of Mexico.

3. The husband of Mrs. Sippy.

Also pronounced *Ippisippi*.

—Janel, age 3, St. Peters, MO. Additional source: Lexi, age 5, Parkhills, MO

Mocch·i·o [MOKE-ee-oh] *proper noun*

The main character of a nineteenth-century folklore story about a wooden puppet who becomes a boy and whose nose grows when he does not tell the truth.

*"Daddy, will you read **Mocchio** to us again tonight?"*

—Leah, age 3, St. Louis, MO

Mo·noch·o·ly [muh-NOK-o-lee] *proper noun*

A board game invented in the early twentieth century in which a player attempts to gain control through the purchase of real estate, earning money by collecting rent from other players whose pieces land on their property.

*"Dad, will you play **Monocholy** with us tonight?"*

—Addison, age 6, St. Louis, MO

mon·go·lia [mohn-GOE-leeuh] *noun*

A tree or shrub of the family *Magnoliaceae* that blooms large, light-pink flowers. Native to the Himalayas, there are many varieties that have been cultivated in North America and are widely grown as ornamental trees both for their beauty and the fragrance of their flowers.

*"I love the smell of **mongolia** trees!"*

—James, St. Charles, MO

Monkeytasking

One day while trying to get my three-year-old daughter, Lillie, to pay attention to something we were doing, she was distracted by the television. I informed her that I was about to turn the TV off so we could complete our other activity. She turned to me and said, "It's ok Mom, I am monkeytasking so we can do both."

—Susie, Lookout Mountain, GA

mon·key·task·ing [MUN-kee-task-eeng] *noun*

The act of performing or executing more than one operation or process at the same time, such as doing homework while watching television.

*"It's okay Mom, I'm **monkeytasking!**"*

—James, age 6, Newport, WV. Additional source: Lillie, age 3, Lookout Mountain, GA

mon·ster·el·la [mohn-stuhr-EL-la] *noun*

A soft, mild, white Italian cheese that is used in baked or cooked meals such as pizza or pasta or can be breaded and fried in individual portions.

*"Mom, can I get some **monsterella** cheese sticks?"*

—Karenna, age 4, Mililani, HI

mo·nun·gous [moe-NUNGH-uhss] *adjective*
Extraordinarily or unusually large, sometimes necessitating a verbal exclamation.

*"Wow, Mom! Aunt Sharon's behind is **monungous!**"*

—Sabrina, age 5, Wood River, IL

mud·dler [MUHD-lr] *noun*
1. A piece of material, such as a scarf, worn around the neck for protection against cold.
2. A device used in the exhaust system of an internal combustion engine to reduce sound.

*"Dad, I think your motorcycle needs a better **muddler.**"*

—Katie, age 8, Rolla, MO

mush·mal·low [MUHSH-mahl-oh] *noun*
A white or artificially colored sponge-like confection made from sugar, albumen, and gelatin that can be baked, roasted, or added to hot cocoa, desserts, or breakfast cereals.

*"Mom, can we get the **mushmallow** kind?"*

Also pronounced *marshpillow*.

—Andrew, age 4, Dublin, OH. Additional source: Kyle, age 2, St. Louis, MO

mys·ter·i·cal [miss-TEHR-ih-kuhl] *adjective*

Emotionally uncontrollable or irrational due to shock or something very humorous, the latter of which is often characterized by uncontrolled laughter.

*"My little brother is so funny it makes me **mysterical!**"*

—Abby, age 3, Mount Pleasant, MI

nag·ra·ta·bag·ra [NAG-rah-tuh-BAG-ruh] *noun*

A word of folklore used in incantations, magic tricks, or illusions for its supposed mystical power.

*"**Nagratabagra!** Now you're invisible!"*

—Geoffrey, age 4, Ancaster, Ontario, Canada

nak·kin [NAA-kinn] *noun*

A small piece of material, usually made of cloth or paper, used during a meal to clean food from hands or face or to protect clothes, one of which usually suffices for each person unless you are eating with children.

*"Mom, I need another **nakkin.**"*

Also pronounced *nackum*.

—Mya, age 5, Ferguson, MO. Additional source: Ashley, age 3, St. Louis, MO

Nas·ty Par·ty [NASS-tee pahr-tee] *noun*

The fanatical assembly of socialist German workers that took political control of Germany in 1933 under the dictatorship of Adolf Hitler and was abolished in 1945 at the end of World War II.

*"Hitler ran the **Nasty Party**!"*

—Roderick, age 8, Bloomington, IL

ne·ces·sa·ny [nuh-SESS-uh-nee] *noun*

Anything indispensable or vital to survival, such as food, shelter, or a new purse.

*"But I have to have it, Mommy, it's a **necessany**!"*

—Evangeline, age 2, Sherwood, AR

neck·y·less [NEK-ee-lehss] *noun*

An ornamental band, string, or chain of leather, stones, beads, jewels, or precious metal, such as gold or silver, worn around the neck, sometimes similar in appearance to a domestic animal's collar.

*"Mom, that dog's **neckyless** was really dirty!"*

—Elaina, age 2, St. Louis, MO

nem·a·lade [NEHM-ah-layd] *noun*

A beverage made from lemon juice, water, and sugar served cold or over ice, making it particularly popular among young entrepreneurs to sell on hot summer days.

*"Daddy, will you help me set up a **nemalade** stand?"*

—Danielle, age 3, St. Peters, MO

net·ter·a·tor [NEHT-tehr-ay-tuhr] *noun*

A person who gives an account of or adds commentary to a series of events such as a story or play.

*"You guys act and I'll be the **netterator!**"*

—Emma, age 4, Madison, WI

New Ears [NOO eerz] *noun*

A holiday honoring the first day of the calendar year, typically celebrated by staying up the night before for the stroke of midnight.

*"Mom, can we stay up for **New Ears** tonight?!"*

—Elise, age 5, Otsego, MN

nin·jer [NIN-jr] *noun*

One of the mercenary agents of feudal Japan, highly trained in the martial art of ninjutsu, who were hired for covert operations, such as spying or assassination. They are characterized by dark and lightweight attire, unique specialized weapons, and their uncanny ability for stealth.

*"You can't hear me coming because I'm a **ninjer**!"*

—Gabriel, age 3, Scott AFB, IL

nock·u·la·tors [NOK-u-lay-terz] *noun*

A handheld optical instrument that consists of a pair of lenses used to view faraway objects at close range.

*"Wow, Dad! These **nockulators** make birds look huge!"*

Also pronounced *binaca-okulars*, *nocanoculars*, and *knockers*.

—Tyler, age 3, St. Charles, MO. Additional sources: Jesica, age 3, Arnold, MO; Jared, age 4, Alton, IL; Taylor, age 3, Belleville, IL

noc·tur·tle [NOHK-tuhr-tl] *adjective*

Active at night, such as certain animals and most children at bedtime.

*"I can't help it, Dad. I'm **nocturtle**!"*

—Emily, age 2, NJ

nu·se·um [noo-ZEE-uhm] *noun*

A structure or institution where artifacts, works of art, or other objects valuable to a society are kept, maintained, and displayed for public view.

*"Dad, can we go to the history **nuseum** tomorrow?!"*

—Kinzie, age 4, Pratt, KS

oat·milk [OWT-mihlk] *noun*

A meal made from ground or rolled oats, typically served for breakfast and sometimes sweetened or flavored.

*"Can I have sugar and cinammon in my **oatmilk**?"*

Also pronounced *eatmeal*.

—Caylee, age 2, Monroe, WA. Additional source: Bailey, age 2, Summerville, SC

Olive, the Other Reindeer

While driving to our vacation destination on the Oregon coast one Christmas, my seven-year-old son, Jacob, was humming "Rudolph the Red-Nosed Reindeer" to himself when he suddenly stopped and looked at me and asked, "Mom?"

"What?" I answered.

"Do you know Olive?" Puzzled and racking my brain to remember anyone named Olive at his school, I finally had to say, "No, honey. Olive who?"

He replied, "You know, Mom . . . OLIVE!"

When I insisted I still didn't know whom he was referring to he finally huffed in exasperation (with that tone that says "duh") and said, "You know, Mom! Olive the other reindeer?!?!?"

—Christine, Hermiston, OR

o•pen ex•press•a•me

[OH-pehn ekks-PRESS-ah-mee] *noun*

Free or unrestricted admission or access, also known in folklore to be a magical phrase or password that allows entry to an otherwise closed passageway.

*"The grocery store doors open when I say, '**Open expressame!**'"*

—Shyre, age 3, Mesa, AZ

o·pe·ra·tu·li·ty [ah-peh-ruh-TOO-lih-tee] *noun*

An instance of optimal circumstance that allows the possibility for something to transpire, such as the completion of an assigned task.

*"I wanted to clean my room, I just didn't get an **operatulity**!"*

—William, age 5, Wheaton, IL

O·re·o Day [OH-ree-oh daye] *noun*

A national holiday in the United States, established for the remembrance of members of the armed forces who died in active duty, typically observed on the last Monday in May by the closing of businesses and schools, the latter of which is most pleasing to children.

*"Yay! It's **Oreo Day**!"*

—Gracie, age 4, O'Fallon, MO

ow·breyes [OUW-bryhz] *plural noun*

The ridges above the eye sockets, formed by the forehead and divided by the nose, that are each lined with a patch of hair that some women commonly trim while other women remove entirely and then redraw them with a makeup pencil for reasons still unknown to humanity.

*"How come Grandma doesn't have any **owbreyes**?"*

—Nicolette, age 3, New York, NY

pack·pack [PAK-pak] *noun*

A lightweight carrying bag with straps that allows it to be carried on the back, typically made of cloth or nylon that also can be colored or decorated, such as with an image or emblem of a popular media character.

*"I have a Supergirl **packpack**!"*

—Evelyn, age 2, Richmond Hill, GA

pa·ki·ni [pa-KEY-nee] *noun*

A two-piece swimsuit traditionally worn by girls.

*"Mommy wears her **pakini** at the beach."*

—J. Love, Abilene, TX

pan·da·cakes [PAN-duh-kayks] *plural noun*

Flat, round cakes made of batter and pan-fried, usually topped with butter, syrup, and sometimes fruit or whipped cream. Traditionally served for breakfast but reported by most children to be even better when served for dinner.

*"Mom is making **pandacakes** tonight!"*

Also pronounced *pannycake* and *pamcake*.

—Leah, age 5, TX. Additional sources: Lillian, age 7, Springfield, OH; Hayden, age 2, Rolla, MO

pants·a·fire [PANTZ-uh-fyre] *noun*

A rubber or plastic nipple for infants to suck or bite on, which often is difficult to keep in their mouths.

*"Mom, Nikky lost her **pantsafire** again!"*

—Grace, age 5, Encino, CA

par·ent·chute [PAIR-ehnt-shoot] *noun*

A foldable cloth canopy attached in an umbrella-like form by a series of straps to a harness that can be worn or secured to an object, allowing a person or cargo to land safely on the ground from the air.

*"Cool! That soldier has a **parentchute**!"*

—Nick, age 5, St. Louis, MO

pas·tra·mi [pahs-TRAH-mee] *noun*

A large ocean wave caused by a seaquake or underwater volcanic eruption that can be devastating if it reaches dry land.

*"If we live on the beach we could get hit by a **pastrami**!"*

—Isabelle, age 5, Colorado Springs, CO

PB and J [pee-bee and JAY] *noun*

1. An abbreviation for the temporomandibular joint that connects the lower jaw to the skull.

2. An abbreviation for a disorder of the temporomandibular joint that may cause a popping sound when chewing food.

*"My brother has **PB and J** disorder."*

—Taval, age 4, Palmer, AK

pea·nut [PEE-nut] *noun*

A "private part" of the male (Daddy) anatomy.

*"Mom, Daddy has a **peanut**!"*

Also pronounced *peanuts*.

—Jonna, age 3

pee·kers [PEE-krz] *collective noun*

Audio devices, typically in pairs, that convert electrical impulses from an amplifier into audible sound waves, such as in a home theater or car audio system.

*"Dad put new **peekers** in his truck!"*

—Rich, age 5, St. Louis, MO

pel·e·quin [PEHL-eh-kwinn] *noun*

A large waterbird
of the family
Pelecanidae, typically
white or gray, with
a long bill that has
an extendible pouch
used for catching fish.

*"I saw a **pelequin** scoop up a fish on TV today!"*

—Michael, age 5, Mission, TX

Penn·sla·va·ni·a [pehn-slah-VAY-nee-uh]
proper noun

A state in the northeastern United States that lies partially on the coastline of Lake Erie, with the city of Harrisburg as its capital. It was established in 1682 and was one of the original 13 colonies, gaining its statehood in December of 1787.

*"I live in **Pennslavania!**"*

—Constance, age 4, Allentown, PA

peo·ple sy·rup [PEE-puhl see-ruhp] *noun*

A sweet liquid made by boiling down the sap of maple trees, typically served over breakfast meals.

*"I want **people syrup** on my pancakes!"*

See also *syreeup*.

—Parker, age 2, Montgomery, TX

pep·per·bal·o·ney [peh-pr-bah-LOW-nee] *noun*

A highly seasoned beef and pork sausage that is among the most beloved pizza toppings of all time.

*"Oh! I want **pepperbaloney!**"*

—Amy, age 4, Maryland Heights, MO

pew·fume [pyoo-FYUME] *noun*

A fragrant liquid or oil, typically applied to the body or clothing that sometimes people use more than they should.

*"Mom, that lady is wearing too much **pewfume!**"*

—Sophia, age 5, St. Louis, MO

pi·a·ni·o [pee-AH-nee-oh] *noun*

A musical instrument with wound metal strings mechanically hammered by white and black keys, usually played with fingers but sometimes played with feet or other parts of the body.

*"Look, I can play the **pianio** with my butt!"*

Also pronounced *panano*.

—Reagan, age 4, St. Louis, MO. Additional source: Mandy, age 2, Ferguson, MO

pic·kar [pihk-KAHR] *noun*

A stringed musical instrument with a long, fretted neck and a solid or hollow violin-shaped body, used to play music by plucking the strings with the fingers, a pick, or other object.

*"Look Dad, I can play your **pickar** with a fork!"*

—Mya, age 5, St. Louis, MO

pink·and·blue [peenk-and-blooh] *noun*

A game played with young children in which one covers their face or hides and suddenly reappears, much to the child's amusement, which can often be insatiable.

*"Daddy, play **pinkandblue** with me again!"*

—Jenna, age 3, Chicago, IL

pink·tails [PEENK-tayhls] *plural noun*

Braids of hair that hang from the head through restraints such as hair bands, clips, or similar fasteners.

*"Daddy, do you like my **pinktails**?"*

—Mya, age 5, St. Louis, MO

pink·wun [PEENK-wuhn] *noun*

A flightless, aquatic bird of the *Spheniscidae* family, native to the southern hemisphere, with webbed feet and flipper-like wings used for propelling itself in water.

*"I saw a **pinkwun** swimming at the zoo today!"*

—Avery, age 4, Vona, CO

pluk [pluhk] *noun*

The soft, moist part of a fruit that sometimes ends up in its juice.

*"I want orange juice if it doesn't have **pluk** in it."*

—Addison, age 6, St. Louis, MO

plung·er [PLUHNJ-ur] *noun*

A person who installs or repairs pipes, fixtures, or appliances that use or drain water in homes and buildings.

*"Mom, the **plunger** is here to fix the sink!"*

—Lisa, age 3, Colby, KS

po·ets·read [POWE-ehtts-reed] *noun*

A form of literature that uses metrical writing to express feeling and emotion, typically using a distinct style or rhythm.

*"I love to write **poetsread**!"*

—Jessica, age 4, Pueblo, CO

poink [POYHNK] *verb*

To push or prod with a narrow object, such as a stick, a finger, or a toy.

*"I'll play, just don't **poink** me with the light saber!"*

—Cyrus, age 4, King of Prussia, PA

pol·ka·nut [POHL-kuh-nuht] *noun*

A fruit that grows on palm trees with a hard, fibrous outer shell, filled with a milky liquid and lined with a white, edible interior that can be shredded and used as a dessert topping.

*"Ooh! I want a **polkanut** donut!"*

Also pronounced *cokeypenut*.

—Oscar, age 4, Arnold, MO. Additional source: Josia, age 3, St. Louis, MO

pol·men·ate [PAHL-mehn-ait] *verb*

To transfer pollen from one flower or plant to another and allow fertilization.

*"Bumble bees **polmenate**!"*

—Raegan, age 5, St. Louis, MO

po·pour·i·ni [poh-puhr-EE-nee] *noun*

A mixture of dried flower petals, herbs, and spices, typically preserved in a porous container or transformed into an oil to preserve or enhance its strong, but not always pleasing aroma.

*"Yuck! It smells like **popourini** in here!"*

—Kati, age 3, St. Louis, MO

pop·skit·tle [POHPP-skih-tl] *noun*

A serving of flavored ice on a stick that allows it to be held while eaten, but only as long as it remains solid.

*"Mom, my **popskittle** is falling off!"*

Also pronounced *pockisull* and *pocksicle*.

—Aidan, age 4, Fenton, MO. Additional sources: Tyler, age 2, St. Charles, MO; Max, age 2, St. Louis, MO

Piggy Shopping Sense

One day when we were probably just sitting on the couch together having a snuggle, my then two-year-old son, Tyler, said, "This little piggy went to Target. This little piggy stayed home . . ."

—Debbie, Camarillo, CA

por·a·do [pawr-AYE-doh] *noun*

A windstorm that occurs over land, characterized by a long, funnel-shaped cloud extending toward the ground, which is as destructive to everything in its path as children can be to any location when left unattended for long periods of time.

*"Mom said my room looks like it was hit by a **porado**!"*

—Wyatt, age 2, Niceville, FL

Toddler Weather Watch

My four-year-old son, Marc, had been developing an interest in the Weather Channel on TV. I'll never forget how hard my husband and I laughed when he ran into our bedroom one night after watching a weather report yelling, "Mom! Dad! There's a tomato warning in parts of Okamona!" Thankfully, we lived in Missouri, but we will never forget that night.

—Sherri, St. Louis, MO

pour·til·la [poohr-TEE-yah] *noun*

A thin, round, unleavened traditional Mexican bread made from wheat flour or cornmeal that is cooked on a flat iron and closely resembles a flying disc.

*"Mom, Sarah threw my **pourtilla** out the window!"*

—Eleanor, age 5, St. Louis, MO

print·zel [PRIHNT-suhl] *noun*

A golden-brown salted biscuit, served either soft and chewy or crisp and made from dough that is usually rolled into a stick or twisted into a knot or other shape.

*"Mom, my **printzel** is a circle!"*

—Molly, age 2, Highland Village, TX

pu·lu bear [POOH-loo-bayhr] *noun*

A large, white bear of the family *Ursidae*, native to the arctic regions.

*"We saw a **pulu bear** at the zoo today!"*

—Alejandra, age 4

puke·un·der [PEWK-uhn-dr] *noun*

An edible fruit of the *Cucumis sativus* plant characterized by its cylindrical shape; rich, green, and usually warty skin; and watery light-green flesh that can be eaten raw, prepared, or even preserved.

*"This pickle used to be a **pukeunder**!"*

—Jasmine Anne, age 6, Annapolis, MD

py·ro·crap·ter [PY-rowe-krap-tehr] *noun*

A person who practices the art of treating misalignments of the joints or the spinal column to relieve certain bodily disorders, such as a pinched nerve.

*"Dad, you should see a **pyrocrapter** for your back!"*

Also pronounced *chirocracker*.

—Rylee, age 3, Gridley, CA. Additional source: Linus, age 3, PA

ra·coon [rah-KOON] *noun*

The protective silk covering that a larval insect forms to encase itself while it passes the pupa stage, such as when a caterpillar becomes a butterfly.

*"Mom, look! A butterfly **racoon**!"*

—Henry, age 4, Tacoma, WA

rai·sin brown [RAY-zihn brohwn] *noun*

A cereal with flakes of bran mixed with raisins, usually served in milk or yogurt and typically eaten as a breakfast meal.

*"Mom, do we have any **raisin brown**?"*

—Ben, age 4, Tallahassee, FL

rain·bow fo·rest [RAYN-bohw foh-rest] *noun*

A tropical forest in an area of high annual rainfall with dense, broad-leaved trees and a unique and diverse animal and insect life.

*"I want to live in a **rainbow forest**!"*

—Ava, age 4, St. Louis, MO

re·larm [rah-LAHRM] *noun*

An automatic device that emits an audible sound or visual signal to cause attention, for waking from sleep, alerting of need, or warning of danger, such as a potential fire.

*"When Grandma cooks she always sets off the smoke **relarm**!"*

—Johanna, age 5, Bellingham, WA

Common Sock Sense

When my niece, Violet, was about two or three, she was getting her shoes put on. My sister, Kristen, asked her if she knew why we wear shoes. She replied, "So your socks won't fly away."

—Kari, Dunnellon, FL

re·mem·bo·ry [ree-MEM-boh-ree] *noun*

The capacity of the mind to recall or retain information such as facts, images, or events. It is a process that tends to be irreversible when wanting to purge information such as when a sibling spoils a surprise.

*"Mom, I can't forget what Megan said I was getting for Christmas now because of my **remembory**!"*

See also *membory card.*

—Derek, age 6, St. Louis, MO

rest·not [REST-naht] *noun*

A business where prepared food is sold and served and can be eaten on location, of which certain establishments are more frequented by parents based on their children's menu prices as well as the ability of their children's menu activities to actually keep children occupied until their meals arrive.

*"How come we always eat at the same **restnot**?"*

Also pronounced *hungry store.*

—Ty, age 3, Brampton, Ontario, Canada. Additional source: Brett, age 3, Fountain, CO

ri·dic·lee·us [rih-DIK-lee-uhs] *adjective*

Absurd, preposterous, unacceptable, or laughable, such as saying there is no such thing as Santa Claus or the Tooth Fairy.

*"Daddy, that's **ridicleeus!**"*

Also pronounced *dikuless*.

—Maya, age 4, San Antonio, TX. Additional source, Kyleigh, age 3, Lawton, OK

ro·bo·not [rowe-bowe-NOHT] *noun*

1. A machine that performs complex, often repetitive, actions automatically, typically as programmed by a computer, such as on an automobile assembly line.

2. A popular style of dancing.

*"Look guys, I can do the **robonot!**"*

—Gill, age 3, Reno, NV

Rock·a·two·ba·ma [ROHK-ah-too-bahm-ah]
proper noun

The 44th president of the United States of America and the first African-American president in U.S. history.

*"Mom, **Rockatwobama** is on TV!"*

Also pronounced *Bomama*.

—Samuel, age 4, Clinton, MS.
Additional source: Sylvia, age 2, Frankfort, KY

rock·y·ol·o·gist [rohk-ee-OL-uh-jist] *noun*

A scientist who studies historic or prehistoric cultures by analyzing artifacts and other remains that are usually excavated from the ground.

*"A **rockyologist** digs up old skulls and bones!"*

—Isabella, age 5, Vanderhoof, British Columbia, Canada

root·beard [RUTE-beerd] *noun*

A carbonated beverage flavored with syrup made from fermented extract of roots, barks, and herbs that almost always tastes better when served with a scoop of ice cream on top.

*"Grandma, can I have a **rootbeard** float?"*

Also pronounced *roofbeer.*

—Sophia, age 5, St. Louis, MO. Additional source: Raegan, age 5, St. Louis, MO

Safe Lou·is [sayf LOOW-ihs] *proper noun*

A port city in eastern Missouri founded in 1764 by French traders that sits on the west side of the Mississippi River, known for its history as the gateway to the Western United States, symbolized in 1965 by its iconic landmark, the Gateway Arch.

*"We live in **Safe Louis!**"*

—Raegan, age 5, St. Louis, MO

sam·mich [SAM-mitch] *noun*

Two or more slices of bread filled with meat, cheese, butter, jelly, or any other combination of food, and sometimes requested with certain conditions.

*"Mom, don't forget to cut the crust off of my **sammich**!"*

Also pronounced *swammich*.

—Rich, age 5, St. Louis, MO. Additional source: Ruby, age 3, Prairie Village, KS

San Fa·ris·co [san fah-RISS-koh] *proper noun*

A seaport city in western California originally named after St. Francis of Assisi, famous for its 1906 earthquake and fire and its iconic Golden Gate Bridge.

*"Will Mommy be coming to **San Farisco**?"*

Also pronounced *Fran Sancisco*.

—Richard, age 7. Additional source: Ruth, age 5, Atwater, CA

san·ta·light [SANN-tuh-lyt] *noun*

Any object that revolves around another object, such as a man-made device that orbits the Earth to collect and transmit media broadcast signals.

*"We have **santalight** TV!"*

—Theresa, age 5, Helena, MT

sap·sick [SAPP-sik] *noun*

A wax-based balm used to keep lips moistened to avoid or relieve dry or cracked skin.

*"My lips hurt! I need some **sapsick**!"*

Also pronounced *chipchick*.

—Lillie, age 5, St. Charles, MO. Additional source: Victoria, age 3, St. Louis, MO

save·an·ear [sayhv-un-EER] *noun*

An object that is kept as a reminder of a person, place, or event, such as a gift brought back from a trip to a far away place.

*"Dad went to Hawaii and got me a **saveanear**!"*

—Sarah, age 4, Indianapolis, IN

sax·o·foam [SAKS-oh-fohm] *noun*

A woodwind musical instrument, usually made of brass, with a single-reed mouthpiece, keys or valves to alter notes, and a flared end.

"I want to play the saxofoam in marching band!"

—Addison, age 5, St. Louis, MO

scram·boiled [SKRAHM-boyld] *adjective*

Mixed together hastily and without order, such as food that has been stirred while cooked in a pan.

"Mom, can I have scramboiled eggs?"

—Ezra, age 2, Troy, NY

scream [SKREEM] *noun*

1. A fixture or device used to provide coverage, shelter, or as a partition.

2. A light-reflecting surface on which images may be projected.

3. An electronic device that displays information, such as from a computer, that children love to touch.

"Dad, Addison got peanut butter on the computer scream again!"

—Mya, age 5, St. Louis, MO

---

sea·force [SEE-forhs] *noun*

A small marine fish of the pipefish family, having a segmented body, a curved, grasping tail, and a neck, head, and snout very similar to a horse.

*"Gramps and I saw a **seaforce** at the zoo today!"*

—Charlotte, age 2, Chicago, IL

shan·ta·poo [SHAN-tuh-pooh] *verb, noun*

1. To wash the hair with a cleaning substance.

2. A cleaning substance for the hair of the head that is feared among most children for its undesired effect on other areas of the body.

*"Hurry Mommy, the **shantapoo** is burning my eyes!"*

Also pronounced *panshoe*.

—Cora, age 6, St. Peters, MO. Additional source: Kate, age 3, Hopland, CA

Shoot·you·bak·a [shooht-yoo-BAHK-uh] *proper noun*

A science fiction character of the family *Wookiee* that is native to the planet Kashyyyk, created by filmmaker George Lucas. The character is noted for its very tall stature, shaggy brown hair-covered body, and a gruff, sometimes warbly, growl-like speech.

*"When Dad gargles he sounds like **Shootyoubaka!**"*

—Daniel, age 3, Memphis, TN

shrump [SHRUHMP] *noun*

A small, long, tailed marine crustacean that is commonly harvested by humans for food.

*"Do they have fried **shrump?**"*

—Berkley, age 3, Nashville, IN

A Necture of Speech

Last week at the grocery store my six-year-old son, Jeremy, and I were in the juice aisle and he asked me, "Mom, does Grandma have trouble talking sometimes?" I told him no and asked him why, to which he replied, "I don't know, I just wondered why Grandma always says she has to drink prune juice to make her vowels move." I laughed all the way to the checkout. People must have thought I was insane.

—Amelia, Fort Wayne, IN

shu·shi [SHOO-shee] *noun*

A small serving of raw fish or cooked shellfish, served over or rolled into cooked white rice, sometimes with seaweed, vegetables, and special sauces. Traditionally a Japanese food, it is also known to be incredibly addicting to Americans.

*"My Dad eats **shushi** all the time!"*

—Daniel, age 6, KY

sick·as·hell a·ne·mi·a [SIK-az-hel uh-NEE-mee-uh] *noun*

A chronic blood disease most common among people of African descent where abnormal hemoglobin causes red blood cells to become nonfunctional and sickle-shaped.

*"Dad, I learned about **sick-as-hell anemia** in school today."*

—James, St. Louis, MO

side·wards [SIEYD-wurhdz] *adverb*

Facing to the side or moving from one side to the other.

*"No, it only goes **sidewards!**"*

—Lilly, age 4, Grand Valley, PA

skel·e·scope [SKEL-uh-skope] *noun*

An optical instrument
consisting of multiple
lenses that can be
adjusted to visually
magnify distant objects
for closer observation, such as
stars, planets, or other objects
that may be in the night sky.

*"Dad, can I look for Santa Claus
in my skelescope?"*

—Delaney, age 4, Nashville, IN

smoke pro·tec·tor [SMOWKE proe-tek-tuhr] *noun*

An electronic device that warns of potential fire by a
loud alarm activated by the presence of smoke, which
can be caused from burning food in the oven.

"The pizza set off the smoke protector!"

—Nathan, age 3, Valdosta, GA

smoke·in·a·troll [SMOHK-n-uh-trole] *noun*

A small, handheld device that controls something from a distance and has a strange tendency to disappear when used by children.

*"Mom, Megan lost the **smokinatroll** again!"*

Also pronounced *gamote.*

—Justin, age 3, St. Charles MO. Additional source: Bryant, age 3, Belleville, IL

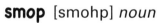

smop [smohp] *noun*

An apron or shirt worn across the front of the body to protect clothing while working with paint or similar substances.

*"I wear a **smop** so I don't mess up my good shirt!"*

—Cora Belle, age 4, St. Peters, MO

sneez·a·ning [SNEEZ-ah-ning] *noun*

Any herb, spice, or salt used to preserve or improve the flavor of food.

*"This chicken has good **sneezaning** on it!"*

—Elliot, age 3, Nashville, TN

snow·boats [SNOE-botes] *plural noun*

Specially designed coverings of leather or rubber worn on the feet for traction and protection while walking in snow or ice.

*"Oh! Look outside! I can wear my **snowboats** today!"*

—Addison, age 6, St. Louis, MO

snow·mow·er [SNOE-moe-uhr] *noun*

A motor-driven wheeled or treaded machine that clears snow by blowing it into the air and out of its path.

*"Dad, there was a blizzard last night so you better get the **snowmower** out!"*

—Kelli, age 4, Mobile, AL

soup·case [SOOP-kayce] *noun*

A handled case with a hinged lid or zippered cover made for carrying clothing or personal items on trips or overnight stays.

*"Dad, I need to pack my **soupcase** to go to Nanny's house!"*

Also pronounced *cutecase*.

—Nathan, age 4, Coopersburg, PA. Additional sources: Eddie, age 5, Las Vegas, NV; Amelia Grace, age 3, Silver Spring, MD

spa·ghee·to [spuh-GEET-oh] *noun*

A small flying insect of the *Culicidae* family, the females of which feed their young with blood sucked from animals and humans, leaving temporary, but irritating, itchy bumps on the skin that are hard to resist scratching.

*"My **spagheeto** bites won't stop itching!"*

Also pronounced *buskeeto*.

—Emily, age 4, St. Peters, MO. Additional source: Gabriel, age 3, Scott AFB, IL

spat·chu·na [SPAT-chu-nah] *noun*

A cooking or baking utensil characterized by a flat end and used primarily for mixing and wiping in a bowl or pan, but may also be used by children as a percussion instrument.

*"I can play drums with Mom's **spatchuna**!"*

Also pronounced *spatcheewawa*.

—Becca, age 4, Shiprock, NM. Additional source: Easton, age 2, Suffolk, VA

spit pea soup [SPIHT pee soop] *noun*

A soup made from dried peas, stock, onions, and celery that is difficult to persuade children to eat because of its greyish-green or yellow color that is too similar to familiar repulsive substances.

*"Mom, this **spit pea soup** looks like a wet diaper!"*

—Maya, age 3, San Antonio, TX

stal·king [STAHL-keeng] *noun*

A close-fitting covering for the foot and lower leg, typically made of knitted material such as cotton or wool, certain styles of which also are made specifically for holiday season when one from each family member is traditionally hung, such as over a fireplace mantle, and filled with small gifts.

*"Look what I got in my Christmas **stalking**!"*

—Mya, age 5, St. Louis, MO

stamp·ler [STAHMP-lr] *noun*

A device or machine that uses a formed u-shaped wire to pierce papers or similar materials and stitch them together. It has also been known to be useful in making minor repairs, such as makeshift sewing for torn clothing.

*"I fixed it with a **stampler**!"*

—Davis, age 4, Fargo, ND

straw·beez·er [STRAW-beez-r] *noun*

A small, red fruit that grows on plants of the genus *Fragaria*, with a sweet and sometimes sour taste that is not only delightful when eaten by itself, but is also a preferred topping and flavor for desserts.

*"Mom, I want a **strawbeezer** shake!"*

Also pronounced *strawbaby*.

—Aaron, age 4, St. Louis, MO. Additional source: Jacob, age 2, Wylie, TX

stunk [STUHNK] noun

A small animal of the weasel family, native to North America, recognizable by its black coat with a white stripe on its back, but more so for its powerful, putrid odor released as protection when attacked or alarmed.

*"Mommy, I think we ran over a **stunk**!"*

—Charlie, age 4, Crystal Lake, IL

suit·brush [SOOT-bruhsh] *noun*

A brush for cleaning teeth, which has also been discovered by children to have many other uses, such as in doll cosmetology.

*"Look Mom, I can brush my Barbie's hair with my **suitbrush**, too!"*

—Tzipporah, age 2, Fort Pierce, FL

sum·mer·bean [SUHM-muhr-been] *noun*

A vessel that is able to navigate both above and below the surface of water, often used in warfare to remain undetected while in transit and armed with torpedoes or missiles, making it especially appealing to young boys.

*"Dad, I want to be a **summerbean** captain some day!"*

—Samuel, age 3, St. Charles, MO

sur·pres·ent [suhr-PREHZ-ent] *noun*

An announcement, occurrence, or object that transpires, appears, or is given to someone unexpectedly, such as a gift.

*"Mom, I have a **surpresent** for you!"*

—Joshua, age 2, Boston, MA

Sus·tem·ber [suhs-TEHM-br] *noun*

The ninth month of the year and the first month of fall.

*"Mom's birthday is in **Sustember!**"*

—Cedrick, age 4, Omaha, NE

syr·ee·up [SEER-ee-uhp] *noun*

A thick, sweet liquid, usually made from a mixture of tree sap, sugar, fruit juices, or chocolate that is commonly served as a condiment for breakfast or dessert and nearly impossible to fully remove from children after a meal.

*"Grandpa, I still have **syreeup** in my hair."*

—Halina, age 5, San Antonio, TX

tam·bo·rine [tam-boe-REEN] *noun*

Any of several varieties of the mandarin orange fruit cultivated widely in the United States, similar to, but smaller than the common orange, with a deeper orange color and a more tart sweetness.

*"Mom, can you peel a **tamborine** for me?"*

—Ethan, age 3, Boise, ID

---

taste bumps [TAYST buhmps] *collective noun*

The small clusters of nerve endings on the tongue that serve as the body's organs for sensing taste, and are also quite sensitive to hot food or drink.

*"Ow! I burned my **taste bumps**!"*

—Sherry, age 5, Phoenix, AZ

tel·e·flone [TEHL-eh-flohne] *noun*

An electronic device used for the transmission of sound or speech over long distances.

*"Dad, Grandpa wants to talk to you on the **teleflone**!"*

—Ryan, age 2, Davenport, FL

tel·e·skin [TEHL-eh-skihn] *noun*

The structure bones that form the supporting framework of a human's or animal's body.

*"I have a **teleskin** inside of me!"*

—Django, age 3, St. Louis, MO

ten·chu·mer [TEN-chuh-mr] *noun*

1. The measurement of warmth or coldness of an object or substance.

2. The most common reason to stay home from school.

*"Mom, I don't think I should go to school today because I have a **tenchumer**."*

Also pronounced *pentochure*.

—Lisa Renee, age 3, St. Claire, MO. Additional source: Erin, age 4, Brampton, Ontario, Canada

tes·kit·tles [TESS-kiht-tuhls] *plural noun*

The part of the male (Daddy) reproductive anatomy that is very sensitive to pain and is more prone to injury during physical activity involving children.

*"Dad can't get up because I accidently kicked him in the **teskittles**."*

—Lucas, age 5, Charlotte, NC

tes·ti·cles [TEHS-tih-klz] *collective noun*

The flexible appendages of certain animals, usually in-vertebrates, used to sense touch or to apprehend prey.

*"I would hate for an octopus to put his **testicles** on me!"*

—Joshua, age 3, O'Fallon, MO

Thanks–and–Lov·ing Day
[THANGKS-and-LUHV-eeng daye] *noun*

An American holiday initiated by early settlers to
acknowledge God's kindness to them, which is now
celebrated at the end of November, typically by a
grand meal with family and friends.

*"**Thanks-and-Loving Day** is my favorite day of the
year!"*

—Isabelle, age 5, Colorado Springs, CO

three·head [THREE-hed] *noun*

The part of the human face that is above the eyebrows
and is the most forward part of the head.

*"Ow, I bumped my **threehead**!"*

—Tanner, age 2, CA

throot [throot] *noun*

A usually edible product of a plant or tree that contains the seed, which is often sweet but rarely as sweet as candy, according to most children.

*"But I don't want **throot**! I want a sucker!"*

—Unknown, age 3, South Bend, IN

toe·man·do [towe-MAHN-doe] *noun*

A specially trained military assault soldier first developed by the Allied forces during World War II that perform surprise attacks and raids on enemy forces.

*"Dad, I want to be an army **toemando**!"*

—Ethan, age 3, Boise, ID

Ahoy Mommy!

One time when we took the whole family out for dinner, we were seated next to a table where a man with an eye patch was eating. My five-year-old son, Eddie, shouted out, "Look Mom, that guy's a pirate!" I just about died!

—Mary, Tucson, AZ

to·mor·ning [too-MOHRE-neeng] *noun*

The day following the current day, usually a reference for up to a maximum of 24 hours into the future, but to children eagerly awaiting something they want, such as Christmas or birthday presents, becomes a reference to eternity.

*"But Dad, I can't wait until **tomorning**!"*

—Jaedon, age 5, Wichita, KS

tram·po·rine [TRAM-poh-reen] *noun*

A hand percussion instrument, consisting of a round frame with several pairs of small cymbals attached to it, sometimes with skin stretched over the top, that is played by shaking or striking with a hand or other object, such as a little sister.

*"Mom! Danny keeps hitting me with his **tramporine**!"*

—Macia, age 4, Bellingham, WA

trum·pin [TRUMM-pinn] *noun*

A brass instrument with a distinct sharp tone, in the shape of a tube usually curved once or twice around on itself, having a cup-shaped mouthpiece at one end and a flaring bell at the other.

*"Louis Armstrong was a **trumpin** player!"*

—Nico, age 4, St. Louis, MO

tu·lip pa·per [TOO-lihp pay-puhr] *noun*

A soft, lightweight, sanitized white paper, usually on a roll, that is used in bathrooms and restrooms for personal cleanliness and potty training.

*"I can use **tulip paper** now!"*

—Daniel, age 3, San Antonio, TX

twen·ty·teen [TWEN-tee-teen] *noun, adjective*

The number after nineteen, the sum of ten plus ten and a favored value of money often given as a gift in birthday or holiday cards.

*"Nana sent me **twentyteen** dollars for Christmas!"*

—Talmage, age 2, San Tan Valley, AZ

Twin·ker Bell [TWEEN-kr behl] *proper noun*

A fictional character from J. M. Barrie's 1911 novel *Peter and Wendy*, who is a fairy that mended pots and kettles, later made more famous by Walt Disney's adaptation of the story in the animated movie *Peter Pan*.

*"**Twinker Bell** is my favorite movie character!"*

—Melanie, age 4, Chattanooga, TN

Ty·men·ol [TIE-menn-awl] *noun*

A brand name for acetaminophen, a medicine used for pain relief and fever reduction that comes in flavored liquid forms for children that they often still will not take.

*"No, I'm fine! I don't need any **Tymenol**!"*

—Harry, age 4, Keene, NH

A Toddler's Alphabet

When my son Jason was three, I started teaching him his ABC's with a picture book. I started by pointing to the picture of an apple and asked him what it was and he told me, then I said, "And what does it start with?" but he couldn't tell me yet so I told him. Then we did "B" with a picture of a ball—same thing. But when we got to "C" there was a picture of a car and I asked him, "And what does the car start with," and he said with a big smile, "A key!" I don't remember laughing so hard as I did that day for a long time.

—Roland, Henderson, NV

un·der·net [UHN-dehr-neht] *noun*

An electronic network that links computers together worldwide, allowing information, communication, commerce, and data sharing, such as video games or items for sale by a toy manufacturer.

*"Dad, there's a doll I want on the **undernet**!"*

—Lilly, age 4, Cedar Rapids, IA

up·chairs [UHP-chairz] *adjective, adverb, noun*

An upper floor of a structure or building, or the direction thereof.

*"Dad, the dog pooped **upchairs**, too!"*

See also *downchairs*.

—Jessica, age 3, St. Louis, MO

V

va·lin·na [vuh-LIN-nuh] *noun*

A tropical orchid bearing a pod-like fruit, often called beans, from which extract is taken to be used in scents, such as candles or soap, or to flavor drinks or food, such as ice cream.

*"Grandpa, can I have two scoops of **vallina**?"*

—Alan, age 5, St. Louis, MO

veg·e·nar·i·an [vej-eh-NAIR-ee-uhn] *noun*

1. A person who does not eat meat for personal or moral reasons, but sustains solely on vegetables, fruits, nuts, or grains.

*"Dad, I am not a **vegenarian**. I like hot dogs too much!"*

2. A person that practices veterinary medicine.

*"But I guess I would be a **vegenarian** if I became an animal doctor."*

—Addison, age 6, St. Louis, MO

Vet·er·i·nar·i·ans Day

[veht-uhr-ih-NAIR-ee-uhnz daye] *proper noun*

A national holiday in the United States, usually observed on November 11, that commemorates the end of World Wars I and II and honors those in the armed forces who have served in combat, typically celebrated with various public events.

*"Are we going to the **Veterinarians Day** Parade today?"*

—Isabelle, age 5, Colorado Springs, CO

vines [VAHYNZ] *collective noun*

The system of vessels that transport blood from the heart to various parts of the body, and are sometimes visible through the skin.

*"Look! I can see my **vines**!"*

—Bennet, age 4, Little Rock, AR

vir·gin [VUHR-jin] *noun*

A particular form or variant of something, such as a movie or a video game.

*"That's the old **virgin**. The new one is way better!"*

—Tommy, age 4, St. Peters, MO

wa·ter moun·tain [WAH-tuhr MOWN-tehn] *noun*

A structure in a pool or lake that projects water into the air, some of which are thought to have magical properties that make wishes come true under certain circumstances.

*"Mom, can I have a penny for the **water mountain**?"*

—Charlotte, age 2, Anderson, IN

wa·ter·lem·on [WOT-uhr-lehm-uhn] *noun*

A large, round or elongated fruit that grows on vines, with a green rind and a sweet, juicy pinkish-red pulp sometimes containing seeds that children love to spit out as projectiles while eating it.

*"Grandpa, Davy hit me with a **waterlemon** seed!"*

—Erin, age 3, Brampton, Ontario, Canada

web·side [WEB-syde] *noun*

A digital location, collection, or series of pages you visit on the Internet.

*"Mom looks at that same **webside** everyday on her phone and laughs the whole time."*

—Davis, age 4, Salem, MA

wind·shi·ples [WIND-shyh-puls] *noun, plural*

Mechanical devices on vehicles, usually in pairs, that wipe rubber blades back and forth against the windshield to clear it during rain or clean it when dirty to maintain visibility.

*"It's not raining anymore, Mommy; the **windshiples** are squeaking!"*

Also pronounced *wimpy-wipers*.

—Patrick, age 4, Las Cruces, NM. Additional source: Elaina, age 3, St. Louis, MO

wi·per [WHY-puhr] *noun*

A cloth or other absorbent material worn as protective underwear for babies or children unable to use the toilet to relieve themselves.

*"Mary needs her **wiper** changed."*

—Franklin, age 5, Reno, NV. Additional source: David, age 2, Richmond Hill, GA

won·der·wear [WUN-duhr-ware] *noun*

Clothing that is worn next to the skin, usually under an outer layer of clothes, but preferred by many children as their only layer of clothing, especially if they like their theme.

*"Can I wear just my new princess **wonderwear** to school tomorrow?"*

—Candice, age 2, St. Peters, MO

yo·gurt [YOH-girt] *noun*

A method of physical and mental discipline from Hindu philosophy, intended to develop control of the body, mind, and spirit, prescribing exercises that often look like one will break in half when performed.

"Mom, does it hurt when you do yogurt?"

—Thomas, age 2, Louisville, KY

yoo·ka·ma·ley [yoo-kuh-MAY-lee] *noun*

A small four-stringed musical instrument from the islands of Hawaii, originally invented as an attempt to recreate the guitar brought there by Portuguese immigrants.

"My brother plays the yookamaley!"

—Phillip, age 3, San Bernadino, CA

yum·my bear [YUHM-mee bayre] *noun*

A small, soft, gelatin-based candy made in the shape of a bear, and available in a wide variety of fruity flavors and colors.

*"I want a red **yummy bear**, please!"*

—Alexander, age 3, NY

My Journal of Mispronounced Words

Alvin Zamudio

About the Author

Alvin Zamudio is an artist, composer, producer, and now a first-time author. He and his wife, Margaret, have three children—two of whom are now illustrators—and live in St. Louis, Missouri. His popular www.americansandbox.com—in part as a result of this book—has developed into a website dedicated to creative and attachment parenting. At least 10 percent of all Alvin's profits—from sales and events associated with this book and his website—will go to support children in need.